To Moire —

NOTHING
BAD
HAPPENS,
EVER

NOTHING BAD HAPPENS, EVER

Joan Fountain

with
Danica d'Hondt
and Stan Zenk

GOLD LEAF PRESS

No portion of this book may be reproduced in any form
without written permission from the publisher,
Gold Leaf Press, 2533 North Carson St., Suite 1544,
Carson City, NV 89706

Library of Congress Cataloging-in-publication Data

Fountain, Joan, 1950-
Nothing bad happens, ever/ Joan Fountain.
p.   cm.
ISBN 1–882723–14–7 (hardcover)
1. Peace of mind. 2. Fountain, Joan, 1950–. 3. Self-
actualization (Psychology) 4. Affirmations. I. Title.
BF637.P3F68 1996
170' .44--dc20   96-26296
CIP

This book dramatizes true events in the life of Joan Fountain. As a dramatization,
certain characters and incidents are composites, but in every way represent real
persons and incidents in the author's life.

10   9   8   7   6   5   4   3   2   1

DEDICATION

To The Creator. Thank you for giving me the opportunity to love and be loved;

To Lois Evelyn Rice—who anchors order, optimism, and balance in my life;

To Chris March, Lorna Fong, and Lisa Shara—for your long-standing unconditional love, support, and patience;

To my "family"—Denise Bissonette, Gary Adkins, Sophie Pettigove, Holly Eimer, and my G.A.L.A. of Sacramento sisters and brothers—thank you for taking me in.

ACKNOWLEDGMENTS

I would like to acknowledge the following for making this book possible:

Fahizah Alim—a warrior woman of words. Your courage creates a light that has touched many.

Curtis Taylor—a man of vision and heart. Thank you for noticing.

Stan Zenk—a gentle and creative spirit. My "soul" brother.

Danica d'Hondt—a woman of passion and inner vision. Your influence catalyzed the critical shift.

Darla Isackson, Jennifer Utley, Richard Erickson, and Paul Rawlins—Thank you for your energy and effort.

READ THIS FIRST

I want you to know right off that I take a lot of flack for something I say. I've said it thousands of times all across America to major corporations like Westinghouse, AT&T, American Airlines, and other Fortune 500 companies. I've said it to small companies and to government workers, to students and to support groups. I've said it in private and over television and radio. In fact, I say it whenever I can and to as many people as will hear me. And you know what? *People listen.* I think I put them into shock with what I say. They don't expect it to come from someone with a past such as mine.

Just look at my "before" photo on the back flap of this book jacket, and you'll see what I mean. Isn't that an enlightened face? I weighed 420 pounds in that picture, and the *tales* I could tell! I went in for surgery once, and they had to build a special operating table and use a crane just to lift me onto it. It's true! But when they laid me down, I suffocated from the weight of my own chest—I forgot to tell somebody I slept sitting up. I have tons of fascinating *fat facts* I could tell. But that's not my message. Too bad—a dieting book might've made me rich!

If you knew the story behind that photo, you might expect me to talk about being a victim of sexual abuse or about marriage to a man who held me prisoner and threatened to kill me. Or about my suicidal addictions to food, drugs, and alcohol. Or what it was like being on permanent welfare and disability because I was too fat to work. Or about a paralyzing fear that made me lock myself up in my house for two years where I prayed every day to die.

What I have to say is none of these, though it springs from all of them. You see, I believe that we sit in God's classroom, and life is our teacher. I refuse to talk about myself in terms of being a victim. I talk about being human and about embracing life. And this is what people don't expect me to say: that I embrace my life *gratefully*. All of it. The abuse, being morbidly fat, the husband from hell, the addictions—everything. All my experience brings me joy and makes me grateful.

Why?

Because I, Joan Fountain, believe *body and soul* that NOTHING BAD HAPPENS, EVER. *Ever!*

And this is where the flack comes in.

"If NOTHING BAD HAPPENS, EVER," people object, "then what do you call losing your job or getting a divorce or watching a loved one die of cancer?" And I get litanies of the symptoms of a sick society: "What about domestic violence, gang violence, teenage pregnancy, racism, homelessness." I've heard complaints on a global scale: "Are you saying that war, oppression, mass murders by evil governments, third-world poverty, and devastating epidemics are not *bad?*"

That's when I point out that I never said nothing *tragic* happens, ever; or nothing *evil* happens; or nothing *unfair, difficult,* or *sad* happens, ever. Tragic, evil, unfair, difficult, and sad happen all the time, and when they happen to us, or to people close to us, it's hard to say these things aren't bad. They certainly *feel* bad. There's not a person alive who doesn't know pain in his or her life.

I've known *a lot* of pain myself. For years, my rather *substantial* body was a clear sign of some very substantial pain! And what's *pain* a sign of? I say pain is a sign of life! I'm here to tell you that pain is *necessary* to life. It was only after discovering the value of pain and adversity that peace, love, and abundance began flowing freely to me. My perspectives changed. I forgave my father for abusing me. And I forgave my mother for protecting him instead of protecting me. I broke free from a controlling and abusive husband, and I learned my true worth as a woman. I quit the welfare rolls, took a job as director of an obesity recovery clinic at a major hospital, and today I run a successful business of my own. I'm no longer afraid of life but feel limitless in who I may become and in what I may accomplish. And all this because I learned the power of four little words: NOTHING BAD HAPPENS, EVER.

After I lost 250 pounds and went on TV, I got calls. "Joan? Was that you I saw on Oprah?" Yes, honey, it was me—I found myself saying it again and again. People wanted to know how I changed so radically, how I turned into the energetic, eloquent, and surpassingly beautiful creature that I am today. (You think I'm *kidding*, don't you . . .)

The answers are in this book. I share them because I know they can give you new vision and help you break through limitations to your own growth and joy.

When I suffocated on that operating table, I died. Instantly, I found myself seemingly at the edge of the universe, viewing it from every perspective at once. In that vibrant moment, I saw that we're all connected. One person's pain belongs to all of us. So does another's joy. When one of us is held back from becoming everything he or she can become, we're all held back to the degree that we are able to help and choose not to.

That's why I share. That's why I stand in front of people and jabber on. That's why people who know me say, "Don't get Joan started!" It's because to tell my story is to heal someone and to continue the healing of myself. And that feels gooooood! So, read on. Let my story flow. Every book opened brings abundance.

PART ONE

▼

EVERY HUMAN PERSON IS AN ARISTOCRAT. EVERY
HUMAN PERSON IS NOBLE AND OF ROYAL BLOOD, BORN
FROM THE INTIMATE DEPTHS OF THE DIVINE NATURE
AND THE DIVINE WILDERNESS.

Meister Eckhart

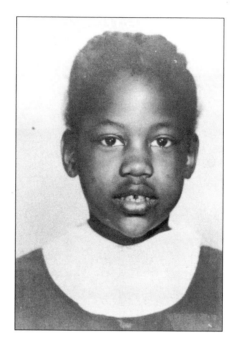

Here I am at age eight, wearing my
favorite red corduroy jumper.

THE BIG HOUSE

One day, when I was a young woman, my momma and I walked together through a renaissance fair in Northern California. We came across a woman dressed as a gypsy who told fortunes for fifty cents. Momma had always been interested in numerology and astrology, so we stopped. Later, when we walked away, Momma must have thought we hadn't gotten our fifty cents worth. A faraway look came to her eyes, and she announced to me in a quiet voice, "Many people will look to you in life, Joanie. You will become a leader, someday." Momma's words sounded right to me, so I answered, "I know, Momma." Neither of us said anything more about it, but I knew it made her happy to see that I had recognized my own worth.

When life turns into a battle, a person's sense of self-worth is often the first casualty. You get slapped in the face, and more than just the skin on your cheek feels the blow. Your ego stings, too, and it stings the worst. It can also take the longest to heal. The major battle in my own life started at age eight. It was my father who fired the first shot. He struck a near-fatal blow, and it took me thirty years to recover. When I did recover, I came to understand that my father hadn't even meant to aim in my direction. I was only a substitute target because his real enemies lay out of range.

My mother outlived my father, and I thank our Loving Creator that her early support of my self-worth outlived him, too. I might *never* have recovered without it.

Momma believed *all* her children had extraordinary worth and looked for every possible advantage to help us fulfill it. We lived on the south side of Vallejo, California—a mostly black area. This was the 1950s, so you can guess that advantages in *our* neighborhood were as scarce as brains in a chicken coop. That's why our living in The Big House was such a rare thing and why Momma took the risks to keep it.

We called our house The Big House because it was once a duplex, but we had taken over both units, upper and lower. Momma had seven kids to raise, so we *needed* a big house. The day the man downstairs packed up and moved out, my mother presented my father with one of her grandiose ideas. The next thing we knew, my father had taken a big sledgehammer to one of the dividing walls! He rigged a set of rickety stairs, and like greedy land-grabbers, we moved ourselves in. Each of us staked out a bedroom, and I found myself choosing the kitchen because it had an outside door. My father tore out the cabinets, but the door stayed. (That door led to some pretty hair-raising adventures once I reached my teens!) We were ecstatic with our new, roomier house. Suddenly we had twice the space. You could actually spit and not hit somebody. It made us feel like royalty.

Of course, in Momma's eyes, we *were* royalty. Didn't matter *which* neighborhood we lived in, she'd say. We were destined to rise to the top of whichever milk bucket God poured us into. And if we spilled over into some other bucket, we'd rise in that one, too. All we had to do was to *believe that we were cream.*

The occupation of The Big House was simply a sign to Momma that we were cream—that even bigger possibilities might come our way. Momma's experiences taught her that life seldom took on a giving mood. A person had to watch and act fast when opportunity came along. And so it was in getting The Big House. If she or my daddy hesitated invading the bottom floor of the duplex because of what the neighbors might say or because we might be ruined without the rent we'd been collecting from the second unit, they didn't hesitate long. Hallelujah! Those walls came down! And I know Momma silently cheered every swing of that sledgehammer.

Looking back on it, I see a lesson here that Momma practiced but didn't put into words. I'll do it for her:

IN LIFE YOU DON'T HAVE TO ACCEPT LIMITATIONS.
WHEN FACED WITH HALF A HOUSE, YOU CAN *ALWAYS*
BUST THROUGH A WALL.

It's easier than you think. Trust me. You just have to pick the right wall, rid yourself of fear, believe with all your might that you are worth the reward, and then let that hammer fly!

3
▼

WE SAW DADDY DANCING

Life is full of unpleasant surprises. I'll tell you, Momma had more surprises in her life than a Pentecostal snake handler with weak faith. I remember one of those surprises. It came one night, late, when Momma gathered up all the kids and took us for a ride in the car. Our car was a big, old late-'40s Chevy, painted sea-foam green and white. Momma had stashed me in the back, and I remember being so small that I could barely see over the front seat.

Somebody asked, "Where're we goin', Momma?" and she answered, "To find your father."

Oh. To find our father. Well, *this* was no surprise. Our father had a habit of staying out late and then showing up drunk. Why Momma decided to go looking for him this night, I don't know. A wife's intuition, maybe?

My father cleaned asbestos from ship parts, and even in his twenties, and before the federal warnings, I think he knew the asbestos was killing him. Sometimes, when he was clearing his lungs at night, the entire Big House rattled and shook. As a black man without higher education, better jobs were scarce for my father. At least his shipyard job paid better than some—but only because it threatened his life to work there. It's tragic whenever men have to trade healthy lungs for a paycheck.

How did he cope? He got angry. Hollered and swore at my mother and us kids. Got drunk with his friends. Spent many weekends away from his family, gambling. He found other destructive ways to cope, too. We discovered one of them that night Momma drove us out to find him.

Momma steered that car straight to the south end of Georgia Street to a darkened bar where my father liked to hang out. She pulled the nose of the Chevy within inches of the bar's big picture window. Then all us kids raised our heads to see over the dash, and there was Daddy. With a woman in his arms. They were dancing, swaying in time to a ballad we couldn't hear a note of. But we could sure enough see. It was like watching a drive-in movie through the windshield, and we'd arrived just in time for the slow-motion seduction scene. I don't know whether or not my father saw our little nappy heads poking up and our saucer eyes staring over the dashboard—we didn't stick around to find out. Something in the way Daddy held that woman made Momma jerk the car into reverse, and we were out of there.

All the way home, nobody said a word. I had the sense that deep down we all knew what Daddy was up to, even those of us too young to understand. But what could we say? We were in shock. Betrayal *is* shocking. It's like lightning—it catches you off guard. Maybe that's why it hurts so much. It's like getting knifed in your sleep.

When he ventured home that night, my father found a box of his clothes waiting on the porch. This was the first of many times Momma kicked him out. Unfaithfulness was only one of

5
▼

the reasons she had to do it to him over the years. But he'd disappear for a few days and then show up again. Momma would always let him in, even though my father never changed. Over the years, he had many affairs, and after a while, he quit bothering to keep them secret from my mother. We kids could even point out a house where one of his lady friends lived.

When I got older, I struggled to understand why Momma didn't kick my father out for good. Today's pop-therapists would diagnose her as chronically codependant—say that my mother required a man, *any man*, to feel her worth as a woman. Others might say that Momma didn't need Daddy, she needed his *paychecks*—what with The Big House to run and children to feed. These conclusions may be partly justified, but I can't dismiss what I know about my mother. Beyond emotional and financial dependency, there was something running through that woman's veins that my father's ugly surprises couldn't shock out of her. That something was *love*. And it meant sadness and betrayal for the wife of Arthur Lee Fountain.

WINSTON CHURCHILL GOT IT ALMOST RIGHT

The story goes that Winston Churchill gave one of his most famous speeches at a college graduation. He was an old man by then, and no one thought him capable of delivering the kind of rousing speech he was famous for. But after plodding onto the stage, he turned solemnly to the audience and after too long a pause, the old bulldog barked, "Never, never, never, never give up!" The audience burst into cheers, and somebody helped the ex-prime minister to his chair.

My mother could have written that speech. How many times could she have given up on my father? Probably more than she'd admit to if she were alive today. But don't assume my momma's life was a washout because she loved a man who did her wrong. Just what do you think the rewards of love are, anyway? That because you love a person, he or she should love you in return? Love is not so fragile a thing. *People* give up sooner than *love* ever does.

Love is like radio waves that move out from a transmitter and just keep on going—through the air, past the atmosphere, out into space: they never end. Well, love waves don't end either. Especially from real, honest-to-goodness love; love you would sacrifice your last good pair of pantyhose for. Once *those* kind of waves get going, they can't be rubbed out. It's a law of the universe. Light . . . love . . . truth . . . intelligence . . . they never die.

This means that if you've loved a person and then later decide you don't anymore, it's too late! Those love waves are already out there, rippling through the universe and circling back. You're responsible for them, you know. Like our Loving Creator, *we are beings of love*. That's why anger, bitterness, and blame damage us. They go against our nature. (Why haven't those angry environmentalists learned this lesson? Makes you wonder what they really *know* about nature, doesn't it?) Sometimes it is best for our own well-being to leave a person we love and move on. But even so, it does no good to harbor anger, bitterness, and blame. Letting only the *best* feelings from the relationship orbit round us heals, nourishes, and reminds us of our capacity to create new love.

I'm speaking not just about *romantic* love—there are a million kinds of love, and so there are a million ways to hurt. To the sensitive and loving person, this world can seem full of emotional fender benders just waiting to happen. The joy in loving must be worth it, though, because there aren't many of us who abandon our vehicles! Momma included.

I'd say that my father sent my poor mother through the guardrail, end over end, and into a ravine! Whether repeatedly taking him back was the best choice or not, I don't know. I would never advise a person to remain in a destructive relationship—especially an abusive one—when a partner's efforts to change are not sincere and sustained. But the choice was my mother's to make, and in the depths of her soul, she loved

Arthur Lee Fountain. She would always see him as the man with the knee-weakening smile, the man she loved from the start—so full of promise and vigor for life that it busted from his seams. But she must have sensed the unresolved emotional issues that made my father feel unworthy and incapable of success. And she must have known that, regardless of his other women, it was *she* who held the first and only *true* place in his heart and that to give up on him would be to deal my father a blow possibly more deadly than the asbestos poisoning eating away his lungs.

Sounds idealized and terribly romantic, doesn't it? Like a daughter trying to paint her parents' image with a wishful glow. But only sad and discouraged cynics would scoff at what I've said. Great joy comes from seeing beneath a person's behavior and finding what's there to be loved. Momma was no hopeless codependant; she was no sucker for a paycheck. Momma had simply let unconditional love find a place in her heart.

Winston Churchill said it right, but I want to add a few passionate words of my own. After all, the old guy himself made quite a splash by mixing truth with passion. Here goes:

> NEVER, NEVER, NEVER, NEVER GIVE UP YOUR WILLING-
> NESS TO LOVE ANOTHER HUMAN BEING. NEVER! FIND A
> WAY TO LOVE—FROM NEAR OR FROM AFAR—AND
> SADNESS WILL GIVE WAY TO JOY.

To me, it seems that good people *never do* give up on things which are good and which are natural to the human spirit, such as love between parent and child, life partners, and between husband and wife. Allowing these to wither is *un*natural to the human spirit—it diminishes the soul and causes sorrow.

9
▼

Nurturing them, on the other hand, enlarges the soul, causes joy, and binds us together in a circle with our Loving Creator, the source of all love and joy.

I SAW MOMMA
DANCING

Momma died twenty-four years later, but never spoke to me about her feelings for my father. His having abused me made many subjects taboo between she and I. It had been that way since the night he abused me. Momma and I became estranged. But as I drove away from her house on the day she died, I experienced something like a vision that spoke to me more clearly than any words. It revealed my mother's true feelings for my father.

The sky that day was dark, and filled with heavy clouds. As I turned my car into the street, rain began falling in torrents. I switched on the wipers and struggled to see the road ahead. Then, before I knew it, across my windshield appeared an image as though projected onto a movie screen. The image was as clear to me as the rain and wipers had been. There, for an instant, I saw my mother dancing. A white and radiant light shone all around her. She was young and beautiful, and her face glowed with a joy I'd never seen in life. She danced, under a blue sky, to some heavenly music I couldn't hear. And she didn't dance alone. In her arms, guiding her gently along, was Arthur

Lee Fountain. He looked youthful and happy and strong. The instant I recognized him, the scene faded, and once again I strained to see the road through sheets of water on the glass. My heart felt warm. The joy on my mother's face seemed to fill my whole being, and I knew this about love:

> LOVE IS YESTERDAY, TODAY, AND TOMORROW. IT EXISTS BEYOND THE BARRIERS OF SPACE AND TIME. SET NO CONDITIONS ON YOUR LOVING, AND JOY WILL GROW INSIDE YOU WITHOUT LIMITS.

PART TWO

▼

WHAT ARE YOU WORTH?

I remember the day my mother told me she didn't have long to live. We were sitting together on the couch in her house, and I wished I could just ease back and get relaxed. Momma never let loose and flopped into a couch or a chair; she sort of perched. So, I did, too, because I wanted to be *with* her, you know. She and I had finally realized we needed each other, and I was always looking for ways to *be* where she was *at*, but our relationship was still rather tender.

"The doctors told me I have liver cancer," she said quietly, but the words didn't seem too hard for her to get out. "They say I'll probably make it through another four months or so."

Remarkably, I could not feel sad at that moment. I knew what Momma believed about life and death, and I knew how I felt about it, so my only thought and feeling was not one of loss. It was more like Momma had just told me she was going to a place that would be different and new. And so I asked, "Are you excited?"

She pursed her lips and shrugged a little. "Well," she said, "maybe closer to the time, I'll be excited."

Whoa! What a thing to ask—*"Are you excited?"* If your mother told you she had four months to live, would you ask if she was *excited?*

Hold your water, let me explain. My momma had an attitude about dying—a sweet, wonderful attitude. To her, death did not mean the end of a person. It meant going home to a world of light and love . . . the continuation of an exciting journey. It meant there were good times ahead!

Momma believed a Creator created all things. All things belong to and all things are a part of this Creator. By my own experience, I know she was right. I believe The Big Guy is the source of all intelligence, energy, truth, light, and love. The Creator *is* these things. We are, too, though to a lesser degree, especially while we're on this planet and inside these bodies. But let this body die, and whoosh, we're out of here, back to our original element. As spirit beings we move on and into another existence, and we continue this grand cycle of learning and growing.

I didn't need to read Betty Eadie's *Embraced by the Light* for proof that our true selves belong to a sphere beyond this world. Something inside me, and inside Momma, already *knew*. But I could've cheered when I read about Betty leaving her body on the hospital bed and realizing that her awareness had never skipped a beat. She was Betty before she died, and she was Betty afterwards. She says if we could only see ourselves as we truly are, we would be amazed at our beauty, intelligence, and glory.

Oh, then somebody please, *open my eyes!* There are mornings I could really use a more glory-filled sight in the bathroom mirror.

But I have never yet looked into a mirror that reflects the honest truth. People can't show you the truth about yourself,

15
▼

either. "Excuse me," you could ask a stranger or your best friend, "would you mind looking real hard at me and telling me what you see?" Whoops. Maybe you don't want to stick around for the answer. Fact is, often the world reflects back to you a pretty screwed-up image of yourself. Sometimes it reflects the opposite of who you are.

Only the One who created you can open your eyes to the truth of your creation. Self-awareness is, first, the awareness that you are God's child—a piece of The Creator—and that makes you limitless in your capacity to gain intelligence, energy, truth, light, and love.

And of course joy, all of which Momma knew and—four months later—had the luck to experience for herself. I know she experienced it because The Big Guy opened my own eyes on a rainy day and showed her to me. And you know what? Max Factor can't even touch the makeover *death* does on a person. My momma radiated beauty from within.

Now, I hope you can handle what I'm going to say next. I hate to be the one to break this news to you:

ONE DAY, YOU'RE GOING TO DIE. BUT, AREN'T YOU EXCITED? THEN YOU'LL SEE WHAT INFINITE WORTH YOU'VE ALWAYS POSSESSED. AND BESIDES, MAYBE SOMEBODY'S WAITING FOR YOU THERE—SOMEBODY WHO WANTS THE NEXT DANCE.

BROKEN MIRRORS

If only we could depend on others to see us accurately, we could learn from their feedback and grow. But many people don't have accurate images even of themselves. Their self-imager—or internal mirror—is cracked or broken. Bad luck, huh? Viewing yourself through *these people's* eyes can be hazardous.

One of these broken-mirror people lived downstairs from us in The Big House—before it became The Big House, that is. His name was Mr. Blackstone, and if you think his name sounds scary, you should have met the guy. I was a very little girl then, and he seemed very ancient to me and very large. And he must have caused strong emotions in me because I can still remember how I felt. He used to watch me play or come home from school. "Hey, Joanie . . ." he'd say and try to hug me or brush himself against me. Ugly, isn't it? Imagine how he felt about himself doing it. And don't say, "Joan, some people just don't have *any* remorse." Bullpucky. Some people have become masters at smothering it.

Now imagine what I felt. I was a little kid. I had no idea what this man's intentions were, but because he made me feel dirty, I thought maybe I *was* dirty. Children trust adults. They interpret adult behavior as true. Since Mr. Blackstone's behavior was true in my eyes, it said something about who and what I was.

A song from the Broadway musical *Into the Woods* says, "Careful the things you say. Children will listen." Cracks and impurities in the mirrors of adults are invisible to children. They accept what you reflect back at them and internalize it.

My best friend at Grant Elementary School was a girl named Sharon Spindler. I think we were six at the time, and we were inseparable. We always sat by each other in class and often got in trouble for whispering. Every recess we played together. We did the hopscotch thing and the hand clapping thing, and we jumped rope and pretended we were Cinderella and the prince. I don't know why we paired up, but we loved each other. We even walked to school and back arm in arm. I lived on Porter Street, and Sharon lived on Sheridan. On the way to school, I'd walk past her house, and she'd join me. In the afternoon, I'd drop her off.

One day, Sharon's mother saw us walking along together. "Sharon," she screamed, "get away from her. She's dirty!"

You might have guessed by now, Sharon's family was white. This might have turned out to be my first painful lesson in bigotry, if I had "gotten it" right away. Instead, a terrible feeling crept over me, and I looked at myself, wondering, "Where am I dirty?" My best friend's mother had called me dirty; I must be. When I couldn't find dirt on the outside, I assumed she meant something else. I suddenly felt unworthy to be Sharon's friend.

Later, I *did* get the lesson, and by then it was impossible to believe that skin color didn't matter. The hard facts of life proved it *did* matter. It mattered very much. So something *was* wrong with me after all.

Much of society still holds up a warped image of non-whites. The good thing is that some of us have grown up now. We don't believe or accept society's reflections of us, anymore.

And that's the key. Grow up. Don't accept others' distorted image of you.

Remember Ed Sullivan and those old TVs we had to adjust by hand? Sometimes Ed appeared kind of wavy-like on the screen—you know, his eyes would be above one shoulder and his mouth above the other. Well, Ed Sullivan was no *alien*. By fiddling with the controls, you could put Ed's face back together. Or, you could choose to leave the controls alone and watch Ed's face do aerobics. And if that were your choice, it wouldn't be Ed's fault.

The message? There are a whole lot of people walking around who need to fiddle with their sets, and that's not *your* fault. Some are so out of adjustment they need to visit Handy Andy's repair shop down on the corner.

Another story. This one's about Peachees—you know, those orange colored folders that have a cheerleader doing pompons on the front and a guy throwing a football on the back. Peachees were a real cool thing when I was young. People in college got to carry Peachees around, and I knew someday I would do that myself. I'd get to roll my socks down, wear a poodle skirt with a real chain on it, and carry a Peachee under my arm around campus. And that's how I knew I'd go to college one day—the vision was *that* clear in my mind. In junior high, I even took Spanish because I knew you had to have Spanish before you could go to college. And in high school I took the classes I'd need for college. By my senior year, I was ready. Not too long now, I thought, before I'd be purchasing my very own Peachee. It didn't matter that by then I weighed 250 pounds.

19
▼

I'd soon look too hot to handle.

Mrs. Seener came into biology class one day to hand out passes for a special assembly. The assembly would be for college-bound seniors only. She read from an alphabetical list the names of the students who would be attending.

"Ferguson, Forsberg, Foster, Fuller, . . ."

Wait a minute, I thought. No Fountain?

"Fife, Garber, Garcia, Gooch, . . ."

I raised my hand.

"What is it Miss Fountain?" Mrs. Seener took off her glasses.

"You missed me. You skipped over my name."

She put her glasses back on and rechecked the list.

"No . . . I didn't skip you. You're not on it."

"But I'm supposed to be. I'm supposed to be on that list."

"This list is for college-bound seniors, Miss Fountain. You'll need to talk to your counselor if you think you should be on it."

"You mean Mrs. Weston?"

"Yes. Mrs. Weston approves all the names on this list."

So I went to see Mrs. Weston—Mrs. Weston of the pale-blue hair and missing eyebrows. Mrs. Weston of the pallid white face that could only be located by the grayish-pink lipstick smears on her mouth. I walked in and she folded her hands across her belly and began creaking back and forth in her chair. She glared up and down at my sloppy clothes. "What is it?" she said.

"I'm Joan Fountain and . . ."

"I know who you are, Joan. What is it you want?"

"Mrs. Weston, there's been a mistake. My name wasn't on the list for the college-bound seniors assembly. I'm supposed to be at that assembly."

"Well, Joan." She spoke slowly. "It wasn't a mistake." She

unfolded her arms and rested her hands on the edge of her desk. "We just don't think you're college material."

I was stunned. I felt my cheeks flush.

"We think it would be best for you to take some home economics classes instead. Maybe you could become a domestic. Because college really isn't the place for you. You just wouldn't make it."

She might as well have held up a mirror reflecting me dressed in a frumpy black skirt, black stockings and shoes, and a little white hat, a bucket in one hand and a scrub brush in the other. Scrawled in lipstick the color of Mrs. Weston's mouth across my forehead would be the words "NOT COLLEGE MATERIAL."

Well, I'm proud to say, I didn't look for too long into that mirror. Nobody was worth listening to who had blue hair and lips the color of a sea bass. I thanked her for sharing, and I went on and graduated from college anyway. And I did get myself a Peachee and carried it around until it became all frayed and torn. Then I tossed it. Another false image down the drain.

At my five-year high school reunion, I ran into Mrs. Weston. I smiled and said, "Thank you for teaching me an important lesson." It was clear she didn't know me from squat, but she said, "Oh, it was nothing," and she smiled back. I just left it at that. I knew I belonged on her list; it didn't matter if she knew it or not. I belong on *every* list of people with stunning potential, *and so do you*. The lesson I learned from Mrs. Weston is to watch out for people who attempt to limit your growth. Limiting growth is an act of aggression against you and against natural law. When tempted to accept the actions of people such as Mr. Blackstone, Mrs. Spindler, and Mrs. Weston, repeat this over and over to yourself:

21
▼

I AM BRIGHT, GIFTED, AND AM VALUED EQUALLY AMONG ALL OTHERS IN THIS LIFE-NURTURING UNIVERSE. THE CREATOR KNOWS ME AND LOVES ME PERFECTLY AND CAN SHOW ME WHO I AM. I WILL LISTEN TO THE INNER VOICE THAT POINTS ME IN THE DIRECTION OF GROWTH.

LOOKING THROUGH WINDOWS

Nanna Eva Evaline Jessie May Mary Turner Dunn was Momma's helper and sometime master of The Big House. Yes, you counted eight names there, and we had fun using all of them when Nanna May wasn't enough. Her husband's name was just John. John Dunn. I don't know what *he* called her. Probably May or Hon or something short because Nanna Eva Evaline Jessie May Mary Turner Dunn was a mouthful—and for such a small woman. Nanna May was tiny as a minute and black as a pen. She was our nanny, and we loved her.

Every morning Nanna May made the rounds from bedroom to bedroom, usually with a dishtowel over one shoulder, screaming, "Eight-thirty! Eight-thirty!" This meant time to get up and get ready for school. Single-handedly, that woman saw all seven of us dressed, fixed our hair, served us breakfast, and scooted us out the door. Afternoons, she greeted us coming home, usually with the same dishtowel slung over her shoulder, and gathered us inside. Momma worked all day long at the shipyards, so it was Nanna May who kept us off the streets. She helped with schoolwork and afterwards read stories to us. Sometimes in the middle of a good story, Momma came in from work, and Nanna May would have to quit reading and go home. How we moaned and carried on!

Especially me. I never wanted Nanna May to go away. As a child, I was happier when *Momma* went away. After what my father did, my mother skirted around me like a cold draft. But Nanna May was a warm shawl to me. She understood the lost and hurting child in me, and she doled out huge gobs of love and comfort and patience.

She well needed patience. At The Big House, I was Jurassic Joan. I bullied the other kids, hid their stuff, broke things. It was like "Keep the chain saw *away* from Joan!" or else nothing would be left standing in the house. Ooh, I could be mean. My pain was too big to carry; I had to pass it around. And then when the fallout settled, I became sullen and depressed. I shut everything out and hid myself in my room. If I curled up tightly in the corner of my bed and became like a stone, I believed I could make myself invisible for a while.

And that was my childhood: from rage to rigor mortis and back again.

Knowing this about me, would *you* apply for Nanna May's job? Probably not, but that's okay—it was *Nanna May* I needed. She didn't ignore me or call me names. She didn't try to talk me out of my emotions or fix me. She just let me feel her love. She sat with me, held me, talked with me about my day, encouraged me, listened. The only nurturing I got as a child came from Nanna May. Her love was deep enough to reach my deepest pain.

It is a rare breed of people on this planet who have the power to make others feel better about themselves. Nanna May was one of them. These uncommon individuals are not like mirrors; they're like windows. They don't interact with a person's outward behavior—they shine their light through to the latent richness of the soul, and they cherish what they find there.

How do they do it? What's their power?

Surely you know the answer by now.

It's the power of love.

Nanna May's love opened a view to the *me* that *didn't need fixing*. And *that's* who she sat with, who she held, who she spoke with, encouraged, and nurtured. That's why I felt healed and why I hated to see her go home at night. She loved me in a way that made me feel worthy to be loved.

It was many years before I learned to see myself as clearly as Nanna May did. For protection I had hurled myself, like Alice, through a looking glass and had become lost in a topsy-turvy world of confusion and pain. To find my way out, I had to visualize my true nature and see for myself that I was not flawed—that *no person* can harm *that* part of me. I was pure and perfect as the day I was born.

You've seen my "before" photo. You've also seen my "after" picture on the back flap of this book. Now hear this: there ain't no before-and-after for the me who never ends. I'm all the same Joan. What you see in the pictures is merely time-lapse photography. But time means nothing in eternity. Just goes to show you that cameras lie, too.

I remember one day, after losing a lot of weight—I think I was down to 300 pounds or so—I took off all my clothes and got a good view of myself butt-naked in the mirror. I got the front view, the back view, and the views of both sides. I thought at first, "Joan, honey, you still got a *l-o-n-g* way to go." Then I looked again. And I looked long and hard, and this

25
▼

time I spoke right out loud. I said, "You know, Joan Fountain, for a woman your size, you're sure a fox!" And I felt so much better after that. I gave myself a break that day and quit trying to fix who I was by fixing what my eyes saw. I determined to accept no more substitutes for myself—no more altered egos. My eyes looked into the mirror, but my heart had seen the light streaming through a window.

It was the same trick that Nanna Eva Evaline Jessie May Mary Turner Dunn worked on me. Bless her soul! She was a tiny woman with a long name and a huge picture window of a heart.

LOVE TRANSFORMS MIRRORS INTO WINDOWS. IT LETS PEOPLE SEE AND BE SEEN AS THEY ARE.

❧ Love means no need to pretend. No need to defend. Sometimes it's love of self, and sometimes it's love of others, but it's always love that draws open the curtains and lets the sunlight through! ❧

THE INUIT EYE

I've weighed well over 200 pounds most of my life. I've mentioned the time I got *down* to weighing 200 pounds, but did you know I was only twelve when I got *up* to weighing 200 pounds? Since age eight, I'd felt this insatiable appetite gnawing at me morning, noon, and night. I was *emotionally* hungry, so devouring buckets of *food* barely even took the edge off.

What's that old joke? You know you're getting fat when you weigh yourself on one of those scales where twenty-five cents gets your weight and your fortune, and the fortune comes out reading: "One at a time, please." Okay, so I was large enough for two twelve-year-old kids. At least I could keep myself company. And why not? I was the only person—besides Nanna May—who was nice to me.

One day at a Sunday School picnic, I'd cleaned up my lunch plate—several times, as I recall—and decided to attack the dessert table next. The table was across the lawn, so I clambered out of my folding chair and headed over. As I got closer, I saw the stacks of cookies and the chocolate cakes, and I suddenly felt famished, as though I hadn't eaten in *hours*. Three ladies in aprons behind the table saw me coming and suddenly became very protective of their goodies. I got barely halfway there, and they started screaming at me.

"No! Get on back there, girl. You're too fat!" they yelled, shooing me with their hands. "You don't need dessert. You've eaten too much already!"

That was *low*. Those women might just as well have stabbed me in the back with a cake knife. Betrayers. *See* how people limit you and believe they're doing you *favors*? I *needed* that dessert to get me through one more minute, one more hour of life.

But these women didn't give a care. The grass was smashed pretty flat under their feet, too. They prevented me from having only what they themselves craved. Like Recovering Alcoholics struggling not to drink, these women were Recovering Voracious Eaters on the verge of taking nosedives into those chocolate cakes themselves. They'd seen me chowing down my lunch and had thought secretly: "Mercy, *look* at her eat. There, but for the grace that other folks might see me, go I."

When people deprive you of something, it's often the very thing they feel deprived of themselves. A worker feels disrespect from a supervisor, so he or she may go home and show disrespect to a spouse. Parents feel hemmed in by tight finances, and they may become severe and controlling with their children. In other words, lack of love begets lack of love, and lack of opportunity begets lack of opportunity. Even when these deficiencies are only *perceptions* they can trickle down to others.

I'm tempted to call this the monkey-see-monkey-be approach to human relations, but this is nothing to joke about, really. When behavior begets like behavior, then the deprived deprive, the demoralized demoralize, the imprisoned imprison, the faithless undermine faith, and the abused abuse.

You'd think that the good graces of love, respect, freedom of opportunity, and individual growth were in short supply on this planet. That they're rationed out to a lucky few somewhere at the top and that only *scraps* filter down for the rest of us—like caged monkeys—to fight over.

The indigenous people of the Arctic, the Inuit, would never understand this.

People often ask me: "What did you do, Joan, during all those days and weeks and months when you were so fat you locked yourself up in your house and refused to come out?" The answer: "I studied the Inuits." And this dumbfounds them. No one understands why an uncontrollably obese African-American lady would lock herself up for two years and study the Inuits. The truth? I was curious. I've always been curious about people and cultures. What impressed me about the Inuit people, whom we used to call the Eskimos, was their sense of abundance. We look out over a vast expanse of ice and snow and see nothing, or at best scarcity. The Inuit sees abundance everywhere. He knows that when he looks out across the frozen land he calls home, he can find everything there he needs for his existence, offered through the great bounty of The Creator.

At twelve, I didn't possess Inuit eyes. Sexual abuse had blinded them. To my view, a barren world stretched endlessly around me, devoid of everything I needed to exist, but especially devoid of love and hope. My mind had blocked out my father's abuse, so it was an unnamed shame that made me feel like an outcast. I blamed myself for whatever had caused my shame, so it felt only natural that I should have to fend for myself across a bleak landscape. Food represented the only life-giving substance I knew. So for me, food meant love, food meant hope, each bite of food meant one more minute of life.

I've known since childhood that homelessness and hunger mean more than being without shelter and food. Many are those who, like me, have wandered across wastelands where cookies and a slice of cake represent false oases. And like those ladies at the table, what little love and hope we're able to scrape together, we're often hard-pressed to share. But the Inuit way is to withhold no life-giving substance—physical or spiritual—from any living being. Symbolized by their giving nature is God's own giving nature. He does not withhold, but only provides. And so must we.

One night, many years after our church picnic, I had a dream about the event. In my dream, everything appeared as it did when I was twelve—sunny day, tables set out on patchy grass, men lolling under trees, kids throwing food at birds, babies drooling dirt—all the same. Only this time, I was there as an adult, healthy and fit as I am today. And the dessert table didn't offer mere cookies and chocolate cake. It practically sagged under a banquet of rich desserts that only a dreamer could dream up: pies of every flavor, cheesecakes, mousse-filled pastries, sugared strawberries, spicy custards. Whipped cream oozed everywhere.

Now, I know what you're thinking: this is Joan's turn for revenge! She's reliving this moment in order to go back to that table and, right under those church ladies' stingy noses, take her just desserts!

Well, not so. In my dream the church ladies had split. But even then, I held myself back from the table, afraid that someone might insult me again and tell me to back off. But then a man and a woman appeared behind the table. They were white and wore geeky-looking clothes—you know, styles from the '70s, all-polyester, that sort of look. Now, when I was a child, our Baptist congregation was all black. I don't recall seeing any geeky white people at our picnics. But this was a dream, I realized, and *anything* could happen—so I resisted pinching myself.

Anyway, in a moment the man came around the table and approached me. He motioned at the table and said, "This is all yours, Joan. You can have everything you want."

Time stopped and the picnic scene faded—everything but the table and the echo of the man's words. I woke up and knew at once that the loaded banquet table represented my life. I understood that there was no limit to the abundance available to me. The first step to receiving it was *to see* it.

The Inuits see abundance. They know The Creator wants us to have all good things. He is our Father and does not deny his children. Can you see that all your wants are *already* supplied? In advance! Don't think for a *minute* that this universe was created deficient in *anything* you might *ever* need for your growth and well-being. And don't consider for a *second* that *you* are an exception to this. You need love? Love is here in abundance. You need hope? Hope is here in abundance. Of every life-giving substance, there is enough here and to spare. You just need to see it.

WHATEVER YOUR PAIN, WHATEVER YOUR NEED, THE PATH TO ABUNDANCE LIES OPEN. WHEN YOU SEE WITH THE INUIT EYE, THAT PATH BECOMES CLEAR.

31
▼

GROWING HYACINTHS

My mother, Halley Mae Noble, was born in 1921, just before the Depression. She grew up in a small town in Texas and had one sister. Momma didn't talk much about her childhood, but if anyone had cause to doubt life's abundance, she did. Momma's mother was plagued by emotional disorders severe enough to hospitalize her from time to time, so Momma and her sister often fended for themselves. When not in the hospital, Momma's mother got by with help from various men who revolved in and out of her life like the recurring flu. How else could she have provided for her daughters? Single, black women had little claim on welfare in those days. Sometimes, for weeks at a time, my mother and her sister had nothing to eat but flour-and-water biscuits and tomatoes. She had only one dress, which she would wash out herself when it became too dirty to wear. Sometimes she'd wear it wet to school because it hadn't dried in time. The place she lived in must have been *no* kind of house, because Momma woke up on many winter mornings with snow on her bed.

No wonder she jumped at the chance to make home improvements at The Big House! But that's the way Momma was. I never knew her to mope around, hankering over what she lacked as a child. She improved whatever circumstances she could and let the rest go.

While living in The Big House, my father, Arthur Lee Fountain, worked at shop seventy-two at Mare Island in Vallejo—a naval shipyard. His job didn't pay enough to support our family of nine. Momma said no to welfare and got busy finding ways to help the family stay self-sufficient.

The first thing she did was to plant a garden, and before we knew it, we were the only kids in the neighborhood that did daily time in a vegetable patch. Momma raised corn and peas, tomatoes, peppers, and beans. We had lots of fruit trees and even kept a flock of chickens in a pen she built in the corner of the lot, which seemed fitting because Momma lived by the Little Red Hen's rule: if you wanted to eat, you had to do your share of the weeding, watering, planting, and picking, or you wouldn't get a crumb. We learned the value of work that way, let me tell you. And we grew up big-boned and healthy from eating all that fresh produce, too. Momma grew herbs for cooking and for teas, and we guzzled gobs of her delicious homemade yogurt. None of us has a shoe size smaller than ten; we are big, strapping kids. So, you know we ate well, and every year Momma shaved hundreds off the grocery bill.

I find my mother's ability to produce abundance from limited resources amazing. Some of her challenges, especially emotional ones, she never overcame. But the part of scarcity she *could* stare down she *did* stare down with that Inuit eye of hers.

Momma didn't earn her high school diploma until later in life, so most of her higher education came from books. Momma loved to read and stacked as many books as she could fit into The Big House. She wanted her children to love reading, too. Besides her books on natural health, gardening, and

33

▼

metaphysics, Momma brought home serious books for us to read like the *Iliad* and the *Odyssey*, Chaucer and Melville, and, if you can believe it, we *actually read them*! We read all the great classics. Momma's collection included every book by Norman Vincent Peale and Emmett Fox and other favorite authors. We even read the books on etiquette by Amy Vanderbilt. At the age of seven, I already knew which length gloves to wear at formal dinner parties.

I used to wonder how Momma knew which books were best to add to our library, until one day she told me her secret. As a young woman, Momma worked for a dollar a week, cleaning the homes of rich white people. Each day, she'd clean very well and very quickly so that she'd have time to sneak into the libraries of those homes and read their books. Our growing collection at The Big House reflected those well-appointed libraries of Momma's wealthy employers.

Today, my love of books and self-education comes directly from my Momma's menial jobs as a washerwoman. Do you wonder why I believe that NOTHING BAD HAPPENS, EVER?

As her children graduated from high school, Momma presented each with a copy of the book she most prized: Norman Vincent Peale's *The Power of Positive Thinking*.

Until the day she died, my momma knew the value of her soul and knew she deserved better than whatever she had at the moment. To the end, she remained self-sufficient, taking responsibility to nurture whatever part of her needed to grow. Viewing life through the Inuit eye is to see that within your own soul lies the wealth of the universe. Scarcity, even in the harshest of life's conditions, is only a myth.

Billions of people, through the ages and around the globe, have been born into what might be called destitute conditions.

My momma when she was in her mid-20s.

But born within each soul is that voice my mother learned to hear—the voice that tells us of our true worth as children of God. There exist forces of oppression and adversity which try to drown out this voice, but the inner voice is not easily silenced. Even in the bleakest heart of Calcutta, India—one of the most desolate of the world's urban wastelands—people have been known to sift through bird droppings and plant the flower seeds they find there. Such displays of an indomitable will to nurture every precious bit of life and beauty have given another name to Calcutta, it's soul-name: The City of Joy.

To paraphrase one of my favorite sayings:

WHEN DOWN TO YOUR LAST TWO PENNIES, BUY WITH ONE A LOAF OF BREAD FOR THE BODY AND WITH THE OTHER A HYACINTH FOR THE SOUL.

The Fountain kids, from left to right: Patricia, Kenneth, Arthur Jr. (in front), Rose, me, and Kathryn.

PART THREE

▼

SUFFERING IS PART OF YOUR TRAINING. GOD IS TREAT-
ING YOU AS HIS SONS OR DAUGHTERS.

Hebrews 12:7

SLEEPING BEAUTY

One of The Big Guy's great gifts of abundance is that he created us all free. (I get to call Him "The Big Guy"—I feel He and I are *that* well acquainted.) Every morning when I get up and realize I'm free, I just whoop for joy! For about twenty-seven years of my life, I forgot I was free. Part of me sort of fell asleep, and very little whooping went on until I woke up again.

My earliest memory is of listening to music from Tchaikovsky's ballet *Sleeping Beauty*. We listened to a lot of music at The Big House because we didn't have TV. Momma used to play records on an old Victrola phonograph she bought secondhand. She'd put on music to entertain us and to keep us out of her hair while she cooked. Come nighttime, soft sounds from the old Victrola lulled us to sleep. We listened to all kinds of music, from classical to Tommy Dorsey, Della Reese, Sarah Vaughn, the Duke, and my favorite, Glenn Miller.

I still listen to music whenever I can. I've wired speakers into my bathroom so I can listen to music while I shower. My favorite bathroom music is gospel—old fashioned or modern, as long as it's up-tempo, lifts my soul, and reminds me of heaven's gifts. Yep—it's me, The Big Guy, and the soapsuds every morning. Like a ritual. Starts me off right and regular—even better than high fiber and prune juice.

But as a tiny girl, sitting in front of that old Victrola, *Sleeping Beauty* was my favorite. The lush, romantic music enthralled me. I remember sitting so still—all the energy in my arms and legs, my fingers and toes, just diverting itself straight to my ears. I listened to each beautiful passage telling its part of the fairy tale, and Tchaikovsky's melodies wove fantastic dreams in my head.

That I loved *Sleeping Beauty* this much seems ironic to me now. I see that I was just like the Princess Aurora in the fairy tale—*before* the fated prick of her finger on the spindle. She was happy and carefree and unaware of the darker sides of life. Until one day, in spite of guarded efforts by the King and the Queen to protect their daughter, the very thing that was not supposed to happen *happened*. The evil enchantress, Maleficent, discovered Aurora's whereabouts and struck her down with a curse. The young princess fell into a black sleep, never to be awakened except by a prince, who must fight his way to her bedside and place upon her lips a kiss of True Love.

As it did to Aurora, the thing that is not supposed to happen to little girls—to *anyone*—happened to *me*. In spite of all the cautious efforts to keep children safe in their own homes, evil sometimes interferes. In my case, it was not a wicked enchantress who delivered the curse, but my own father.

One day the whole family gathered to the kitchen for a family counsel regarding household chores. Everyone started arguing and trying to strike bargains over who should be assigned to which chore. In the middle of all this yelling, my father just grew quiet and began staring at me. Then he said, in a loud voice, "Of all my children, Joanie is the prettiest."

It was a strange thing to say during an argument over job

39
▼

assignments, and it silenced everyone. Panic crept into my stomach. These were *not* words I wanted my brothers and sisters to hear. I had to live with these kids, bunk with them, eat and even bathe with them. Mean stuff was known to happen at The Big House when one kid got favored over another. Had my father said this to be mean? Was he joking or what? During the silence, he repeated that of all the children, I was the prettiest, and my panic turned into something closer to terror. I realized that my father *had* meant to hurt me, and what could a girl of eight make of that? I felt the look in his eye trying to trap me somehow, and I wanted to run out of the room. But somebody began arguing about chores again, and my father turned his attention away.

40

▼

Whatever my father began that day, he soon completed. It was only a few nights later when he abused me. And similar to the Princess Aurora (who, the instant the spindle pricked her flesh, fell fast asleep), my own awareness slipped me away into a dreaming-place the moments during the abuse. It would be many years before I would consciously confront the horrifying realities of incest.

My memories of that night stayed locked inside that dreaming-place for twenty-seven years. But I began living the effects of the incident starting the morning after. I woke up feeling like a stranger in The Big House—feeling like a stranger inside my own body. My injuries were painful, and they mystified and frightened me. I didn't understand how I had injured myself *there*. My mother wouldn't explain, and I was too afraid to ask. She seemed as silent as stonework towards me—and as uncaring. The doctor ordered sitz baths to help me heal, so Momma left me sitting for long periods naked in shallow pans by the living-room heater. Over the next several days, my brothers and sisters made wisecracks and laughed at the sight of my brown butt showing in public, but Momma didn't try to shut them up or to rescue me. She didn't even protect me when my father joined in the teasing. If she treated me with indifference, then my father treated me with disdain. He said cruel things to me, called me names, and said I was trash. And sitting there naked and shivering in that dirty dishpan, I believed my father. I *felt* like trash—filthy and scummy and despised like trash—but I didn't know why. Shame had fallen on me like hot tar and had changed me into something detestable. I was no longer the little girl who loved music and believed life to be full of romance and happiness. That part of me had fallen into a dark slumber and would be stuck there until a day when True Love would come along to wake me up.

But what would I wake up *to*? A juicy kiss and Happily Ever After in the arms of a buff and wealthy prince? Only on the soaps! No, this sleeping beauty would wake up to the memory of what had happened that night at The Big House. I would recall those details. I would know the hidden secret behind my shame. And you know what? I'm glad I stayed asleep for twenty-seven years. I would never go back to that sad, little dishpan girl and whisper into her ear even one word of the truth about the abuse that I know today. Would you?

We say that the truth makes us free, but sometimes that freedom is more painful that being uninformed. Some truths cause more pain than a person can bear until they become stronger and more mature.

I've seen people, fatter than I've ever been, at fast-food places. They order those super-meal deals, extra everything, and they don't bother to have it wrapped or bagged, 'cause they just pull up to the drive-through with their mouths open. I

41
▼

want you to know that when I see these people, I feel their pain. I've been there. I know about burdens too hard to bear. I look at that guy with both fists wrapped around his triple-cheese, all-fat-patty burger, and I don't begrudge him that burger. It's the only thing he has right now to help him cope with pain. At least it's not the barrel of a gun he's trying to swallow.

People heal better when they're alive, you know; sometimes they just need time. It's different for each of us, but for myself, I know I could not have survived knowing the truth about my abuse any sooner than I learned it. I might have gone insane, tuned my channel permanently to signals from outer space, or I might have taken my life. To be free from the truth for a while was a blessing. But we can't sleep forever. One day, we all have to wake up and smell the skunk cabbage.

Once The Creator knew I could manage the pain of being fully aware, he woke me up with a kiss of True Love. Have you heard that gospel song by The Wynans where they sing: "Millions didn't make it, but I'm one of the ones who did"? Well, that's me! I sing it often in the shower, and I weep for joy because God woke me up in my right mind. I've got all my fingers and toes, and life is truly a miracle. This Sleeping Beauty's had her curse reversed. You can just call me Beauty now.

TRUE GROWTH OCCURS WHEN YOU ARE FREE—NOT FROM THE TRUTH, BUT FROM YOUR OWN NEGATIVE RESPONSES TO THE TRUTH.

DENIAL IS NOT A RIVER IN EGYPT

Our Creator placed inside each person a spark of something that won't be lied to. Call it conscience, moral sense, or whatever, but encoded into us is the irrepressible need to stick to the truth. Veer away from it, and all havoc breaks lose. Our bodies rebel, go haywire; we get anxious, irritated, even angry. Remember those ladies at the picnic—the ones that got "the fear of the flab" put into them at the sight of me? I was truth on two legs that day, and I filled those ladies with nervous energy. To rid themselves of it they had to yell and scream at me that *I* was too fat.

Fact: ten out of ten psychiatrists agree that people ridicule in others the truths they want to deny in themselves. If you counted noses of the too-fat females at the picnic that day, I say you'll get an answer greater than *one*.

Want to keep your blood pressure low? Stick to the truth—every bit of what you are able to recognize. Lie detectors work by measuring variations in blood pressure, heart rate, breathing, and the way the skin conducts electricity between when a person tells a lie and when he or she tells the truth. Dodging the truth is not natural. Whenever we do it, our body sends up an alarm—even when the truth we attempt to evade is an unpleasant one. My father's abuse was so *terrifying* that my conscious self had to deny it to avoid going looney-tunes. But denial is denial is denial. And it *ain't* a river in Egypt, honey. Dip your toes into denial and you'll suffer worse consequences than soggy toe jam.

Denial causes a gnawing feeling inside, and as a child I mistook that feeling for hunger. No surprise then that soon after the abuse, I started putting on weight. I stuffed myself at meals and smuggled leftovers to my room—which happened to be a former kitchen, remember. No coincidence there! I honored the spirit of the space and stockpiled bread, donuts, crackers—anything I could filch from the kitchen upstairs. I'd sneak up there late at night and bring back armloads of food. I enjoyed many clandestine feasts in the dark of my room. Momma finally had to fit the refrigerator and the cupboards with locks, but that didn't stop me. I learned how to pick them. I even figured out how to remove the hinges from cabinet doors to get at food because I *had* to eat. It felt good to nourish myself when no one else seemed to care. Just to have food *near* soothed and comforted me. I learned that chewing and swallowing occupied my senses so that I didn't have to think or to feel. But no matter how much I ate, I could not satisfy the ache inside and every morning I got out of bed a little wider than when I got into it the night before.

At school the kids yelled, "Hey, you cow!" My father and my brothers and sisters called me "fat pig" or "ugly hippo," and I wondered why fat girls reminded people of animals. But at least I got a little attention, which is better than being ignored. Besides, I wanted to be fat. I wanted to be ugly. I wanted desperately to be anything but the prettiest. I accepted the name-calling, just so long as nobody ever tried to *touch* me.

See how clearly the truth shows itself? The thing I feared the most was to *be touched*. I had no conscious memory of anyone touching me to hurt me. Momma spanked us, but the hurt never lasted long. And though my father used the rankest language on us, even dead drunk he never beat us. So why my fear? *This* is what I'm *telling* you: you can't suppress truth! It *always* manifests itself in the body—you just have to know how to read it. I was so afraid of getting touched that in high school I hid until the halls cleared so that I could make it to class without being brushed against. I racked up an impressive tally of tardies doing that.

All through school, I continued fortifying myself with layers of protective fat. I learned that food shielded me from harm, not by making me larger, but by making me smaller and smaller as I retreated behind an ever-growing barrier of flesh. Soon I would be so small inside my fortress that nobody could ever find me, and I would be safe at last.

But this was a lie. No matter how fat I got I still felt vulnerable. And on top of that, I experienced all the side effects of obesity. I had no friends, never went on a date, had to wear ugly dresses my momma made because no store carried my size, got teased mercilessly at school and at home. Can you blame me if I turned to alcohol sometime during my teens? I started hanging out with this girl, Caroline. She was overweight, too, and she was twenty-one and could buy booze. We turned my kitchen-bedroom into a private bar, complete with bourbon, scotch, vodka, and even bar glasses that we stole from somewhere. Every day after school, Caroline and I got drunk together in my room. I didn't know it, but Caroline was

45
▼

just the buddy I needed to support me in my denial. Sometimes other kids joined us, not for our company, but for our booze. My mother knew about our drinking but never seemed to care. I wanted to tell her why I drank. That I felt dirty, bad, and wrong for this world. That I needed things filling, numbing, or entertaining enough to distract me from pain. But Momma had long ago quit noticing.

At my high school graduation ceremony I weighed almost 300 pounds. You know, they don't make those robes quite large enough for some people. But I did have a specially made uniform so I could play in the band. Some cutup in the clarinet section changed the title of my music to read "Plump and Circumstance."

Today, it is well known by scientists and health professionals that the mind and the body are two halves of the same system. Many changes in the ways physical and mental illnesses are treated reflect this view. A newer area of research, one which attracts many skeptics, goes a step further. It assumes the existence of a third part to our beings: the spirit. I've always believed that the mind, the body, and the spirit comprise the whole of who we are. I also believe that within our spirit resides the light of truth. This light suffuses and informs the body and the mind. When we attempt to go against it, we can get sick— mentally and physically. Truth is a universal element that can't be altered or destroyed. You and I are like tiny flies banging our heads against a windowpane when we oppose it. Something has to give, and it won't be the glass.

In this day of natural foods, natural fibers, natural toilet bowl cleaners, and natural everything else, I figured *somebody* ought to warn people about one of the most toxic elements ever known.

WARNING: DENYING OR OPPOSING THE TRUTH CAN
HAVE PAINFUL AND EVEN LIFE-THREATENING EFFECTS IN
HUMANS. ENGAGE IN EITHER AT YOUR OWN RISK.

NO COINCIDENCES

I've suffered at the hands of two men in my life. You know about the first—a man who pretended to be a father. Well, later came Jerome, a man who pretended to be a husband. I think about Jerome (only when my thoughts run truly errant), and I wonder how many of us women suffer from the mutant genetics that make us attractive to stupid men. Poor Jerome. The man's lips moved while he read. Normally, this isn't something to laugh at in an adult, but Jerome's lips moved *s l o w l y* and, I swear, to the syllables of some alien language. But hold that thought (if you can bear to) while I set up the Jerome story with a different one. This story has to do with that geeky white couple from my picnic dream—the ones who offered me everything on the dessert table. In that dream is not the only time I've seen this couple. I had a *real-life* encounter with them one day, shortly after I met Jerome.

When I got skinny (now don't get mad and slam this book shut—I promise to tell you later how I accomplished this), I worked as the director of the Obesity Recovery Clinic at a local hospital. It was a period in my life when I had a real attitude about myself because of my hot new bod and my hot new job.

One day I had an appointment with a producer to discuss a

TV commercial I wanted to make for the Clinic. I had to drive to the Java City coffee shop at 19th and Capital downtown—which I hated because the price for a parking place downtown is three Excedrin headaches and one panic attack. But I thought it *way cool* to do business with a TV producer at a coffee shop, so I went.

Thankfully, luck—or something else—was with me that day. On my second trip around the block I snagged an empty slot just beyond Java City. Perfect! All my poise intact, I grabbed my slim-line briefcase and stepped out of the car. Then I noticed this elderly man and woman I'm telling you about walking slowly along the sidewalk toward Java City. I couldn't help noticing their clothes. The old man wore a plaid shirt and striped pants that left a wide, pale-flesh gap above his socks, and Hush Puppies. His getup was all-polyester—I noticed it right off. (Hey! So I have this *thing* against wearing petro-chemicals, okay?) The woman's dress was all flowery and faded. She looked like a hippie with a Geritol deficiency.

The two shuffled along in no kind of hurry, so I stalled getting myself to the sidewalk. I wanted them to walk on ahead because they seemed like the type that might stop and talk to me, and I was afraid they'd give me verbal cooties, if you know what I mean. (Ooooh. Judgmental Joan!) Besides, as I said, they were dressed *really badly* and I was looking so cool that day in a sleek white skirt with a slit up the front, a red blouse, and red pumps with three-inch heels—linen, silk, and leather; *all-natural* fibers—and I just refused to mix socially with *geeks*.

Luckily, they went by without stopping and continued past the coffee shop door. Relieved, I headed for the door myself when—*split my pantyhose*—if those two geeky white folks didn't end up *behind me* somehow! They caught up to

49

▼

me, and the man chirped in a friendly tone, "Would you like a Bible?" The woman just stood there, not saying a word while the man produced a little Gideon Bible from a pocket or somewhere.

I didn't have a Bible in my house at the time—I just never thought to get one. But a feeling from deep inside told me that I ought to get one now. I said, "Yes," and accepted the Bible from him. I felt intense relief spread through me, and I just stood there, stunned for a moment, staring at the book in my hand. I thought I should thank the couple, but when I looked up, they were gone!

Now, I'm talking *real life* here. This wasn't a dream. That man and woman were *there*, and then they *weren't*. I blinked a few times and tried to figure out how they had scampered around the corner so fast—they hadn't seemed that healthy to me. I slipped the Bible inside my briefcase and entered Java City for my appointment.

What do you think of that? Twice, this couple has come to me with something I needed. Once, to give me a Bible which would one day save my life, and again, to give me a message that opened my eyes to the limitless possibilities in my life.

My faith tells me that these people are angels. Yes, I *do* believe in angels. I believe that the Lord touches our lives in many direct ways and that it's important to recognize His touch when it comes. I know people who credit every success to themselves, to their own abilities, or to luck or coincidence. But to tap into the abundance of life is to tap into the abundance of The Creator of life. To miss this connection is to miss the reasons behind success. Our experiences come to us in ways that best allow us to grow. We need to examine success in that light and try to see the lessons we're meant to learn from it.

I believe people have guardian angels. I have geeky white ones. I've learned from what they've given me, and I've also learned from their having come to me at all.

THE CREATOR NEVER GIVES SOMETHING WITHOUT A REASON. AND THE MANNER IN WHICH HE GIVES IT IS NEVER ARBITRARY.

GIDEONS TO THE RESCUE

Blind dates are everything they're cracked *down* to be. That's how Jerome got into my house. A janitor at the Obesity Recovery Clinic, Lee, set us up.

"You're a nice lady," Lee said to me one day. "You should be seeing someone."

People told me this all the time, and maybe I was ready to start listening. I had money, a house, a career. All I really lacked was *a husband.* (Oh, boy. I bet you can see what's coming. There's this pecking order among women, see, and I didn't want to end up a *spinster*. A spinster is really *down* there, you know, but a wife is *up* there. And even a *divorcee* is better than "nobody ever asked." I'm afraid I fell for the old lie that a woman without a man is not much of a woman—so you don't need to wonder for whom the bell tolled . . .)

"I know this great guy, Jerome," Lee went on to say.

"Yeah?" I said. "What's he do?"

"He works over at Valley Creamery. He drives one of their big delivery trucks."

"Oh . . ." Downer. Remember, I had this posh job. I also

had an *attitude* about men who worked *below* my own corporate level.

"But he used to play pro football."

"Really?" Maybe I was interested after all. *Pro* sounded pretty high up on the corporate ladder to me.

"He got hurt or something. I don't know," Lee said.

At those words, maternal instinct—every woman's enemy when it comes to men—started making my stomach flutter. "Oh, that's too bad . . ." Maybe this man needs me, I thought. An ex-football player, hmmm . . .

A couple of months later, Jerome and I were married in a little wedding chapel by the shores of Lake Tahoe—but *don't* go wasting any Kleenex crying over a happy ending. Whenever I remember the fact that I actually said "I do," I want to make tracks to the nearest bathroom and say a word or two to Ralph on the big white phone.

I'm sorry to say something this shocking, but the nicest thing Jerome ever did for me was to hit me in the mouth hard enough to make my lip bleed. That way, when I called 911 and the police showed up, they found blood on my face and took him away. Otherwise they wouldn't have done a thing. Of course when I made that call, I had to pretend I was calling my sister, otherwise he would never have let me touch the phone.

It took me a long time to figure out why I married Jerome because he acted exactly like my father. It's scary to think I could have been *that* stupid! He was an alcoholic with an uncontrollable temper. Temper, *khh!*—he was a human *flamethrower*; touch his button and he'd scorch you in a second. Something on TV could send him into a rage. On one of our dates, he plunged into a street fight with some guys who used a foul word within my range of hearing. Jerome was drunk, and

53
▼

the two guys beat him to a pulp. On the night of our engagement party he had a fight with one of his friends on the front lawn of my own house. My mother was even there to see that. I mean, I had plenty of warning, and I still married him.

By this time I had become a professional counselor, and my success in that field gave me confidence that I could fix Jerome. He came from an abusive background, had an absentee father, and a mother who dealt with her own pain by taking in any man with two legs. No surprise then that his drinking habit began at an early age. His dreams of a football career plummeted when he ripped up his knees during training. Jerome was no ex-pro; he was no ex-anything. He was an overweight diabetic on insulin and a mean SOB with a drinking problem and no desire to change. He made the perfect subject for a good rescuer to come in and try to save.

Enter Joan Florence Nightingale Fountain.

The truth is, I really thought I *could* change him. And when he wouldn't be changed, I felt that I just hadn't tried hard enough, so I stuck by him.

For Jerome's part, he saw me as this angel on a pedestal, but because he felt so low, he had to tear me down in order to feel worthy of me. He screamed at me and berated me in the most unspeakable terms. If I ever spoke back, he'd hit me. But the next day he'd say, "I'm sorry, I'm sorry, I'm sorry," and I'd think, I can fix him, I can fix him, I can fix him, and wonder if maybe I held some of the blame for his behavior. Talk about a deadly cycle of abuse and codependency! *Jerome fell down and broke his crown and Joan came tumbling after.*

In the end, I wouldn't be alive today if not for a book that saved my life. You guessed it—the little Gideon Bible I got from my geeky friends. I suffered many terrifying nights with

54
▼

Jerome on the rampage. I had this little spot on the kitchen floor where I'd sit and read that Bible while he bellowed insults at me. He paced the room, gripping a liquor bottle, and, with bitter and ugly words, reviled my profession, my womanhood, my body, my reputation, anything about me he could think of. I sat there calmly and read. This went on for hours—sometimes until three or four in the morning, and I'd have to get up and go to work the next day. He'd get angry and slap the Bible out of my hands, and I would crawl to get it, crawl back, and continue reading. He'd slap it away again, and I'd quietly crawl and get it. Sometimes, Jerome got tired and sat down. I'd think, oh, good, I can sleep, and I'd close the Bible and doze off. Then he'd hit me to wake me up, and off he'd go again.

I knew what Jerome wanted. He wanted me to get mad, yell back at him, or fight. But if I had, he would have killed me. He would have turned berserk and then all 280 pounds of him would have just launched at my throat. He was a sick, sick person. He transferred everything he hated and wanted to kill in himself onto me. But what kept me calm, kept me from defending myself, was that Bible—those words of love and comfort and peace. Love your enemies, the Master taught. Pray for those who despitefully use you. The meek shall inherit the earth. The words flowed through me, around me, quieted me, gave me strength. Night after night, through the weeks and months, the little Bible kept me sane and kept me alive.

And then came the night he hit me in the mouth with his fist, and the police took Jerome away. I had finally seen that I would not be the person to change him. Since I was financially secure and there were no children, I lost no time in filing for divorce. I said, "May the screen door hit ya where the good Lord split ya," and Jerome never again stepped foot in my house.

55
▼

Do I believe in angels? Oh, *yes*. And I still have my little Bible. It proves to me that our experiences are meant to help us grow, not to destroy us. If a way to end our adversity can't be found, help will be provided to see us through. That help may not come in so obvious a way as visits from angels. Often, we never know how we get ourselves out of the scrapes we get ourselves into or how we find strength to endure our continuing trials. But I *know* that support *does* come. God made this message perfectly clear to me by sending a couple of very obvious, goofy-looking, polyester angels my way. He knows that, with me, subtle hints don't work. Here's the message:

GOD NEVER ALLOWS PEOPLE TO BE CHALLENGED TO THEIR LIMITS WITHOUT ALSO PROVIDING A WAY TO HELP THEM TO ENDURE.

FEAR'S BACKHOE

Fear is a backhoe that carves giant potholes in the road of life. And guess who sits behind the wheel? You do. Jerome was one of the biggest potholes in my life. I dug it out of fear, and I dug it so deep I almost died getting out of it. It was stupid to marry him and stupid not to divorce him sooner. Sometimes I wish I could beam my voice up to the biggest satellite in space and scream down to every person on earth:

BEWARE! FEAR MAKES YOU STUPID!

So what was I so afraid of that made me want to marry Jerome? I was afraid people would think less of me if I were successful at everything but love. I feared my career might suffer if those I wanted to impress saw I couldn't get a man. I feared that men wouldn't find me attractive so I'd better latch on to the first one who did. I feared I might end up alone for the rest of my life. I feared that without a man to protect me, I was vulnerable—I might get taken advantage of or abused by other men. I feared that missing a husband made me incomplete, like missing a leg or an arm or something.

Hah! Why couldn't I see that when I married Jerome I was missing my head?

Here's something else you should know about fear:

FEAR PUSHES YOU HEADLONG INTO THE VERY THINGS YOU'RE AFRAID OF.

Let me prove my point.

I was afraid people would think less of me if I didn't marry. Do you think people thought *more* of me for marrying Jerome? I mean this guy's favorite outfit was a burgundy, polyester *leisure suit*, for heaven's sake. And do you think I, Joan, who had recently become a high-fashion snob felt proud to introduce my Polyester Hunk to people in my profession? I'd rather have picked my nose in front of them during dinner.

My fears of being unattractive came true. The stress showed on me. I got no sleep, and I had dark splotches where Jerome hit me. Marrying him brought on the very abuse I had feared.

As far as my fear of living alone, I would never be more alone in my life than during those long nights in the kitchen when only my little Bible saved me. I actually prayed for the gift of being alone again.

So why didn't I divorce Jerome sooner or at least tell somebody that he was abusing me and get help? Fear. I didn't want others to discover what I *stupidly* thought I could hide—that I had made a really, really *stupid* mistake. I was too embarrassed to ask for help. It took a fist to the mouth to finally make me *unstupid* enough to save myself.

You know, I didn't deserve the gift of that little Bible. But God sends his grace no matter how stupid we get. I thought I could fix Jerome, but only The Creator can fix his children. My marrying Jerome was The Creator's way of fixing my fears. NOTHING BAD HAPPENS, EVER, remember? I'll never be afraid to *not* marry again!

I used to be afraid of flying, too. Now, my career sends me across the skies from coast to coast. God fixed *that* fear, too, didn't he? Now, at the beginning of every flight, I don't even break a sweat when the flight attendants do their "safety dance." I've flown enough to know they're not predicting my future.

You will never feel so free as you will on the day you are free from fear. Jerome's small step out my door became one giant leap for Joankind. I felt safe again. I felt confident. I felt strong. Yes, I dug a massive pit for myself. But I learned a lot about myself as I climbed back out. I learned not to repeat the mistakes I'd made out of fear.

59
▼

This is what I do now when I feel afraid: I stop. I identify my fear. I remind myself that no fear is rational in a child of The Creator. Next, I go find whatever I'm missing that makes me afraid. If it's courage, I gather some. If it's knowledge, I learn what I need to know. If it's energy, I take better care of my health. If it's self-image, I go shopping! And when I'm prepared, I walk straight at the thing I fear and go right on through it. Then I calm myself and say, "That wasn't so bad, now, was it? Next time don't be such a ninny."

So, heed my advice all you hard hats out there. Get *down* off that backhoe of fear! You won't get anywhere until you do. Kill the ignition and throw away the key! *Quick.* Before you do something really stupid.

DOWN AN UPWARD PATH

I've learned that freedom has two parts. First, the freedom to make choices, and second, the freedom to implement what one chooses.

The first part of freedom is an unalienable right that no one can take away. They can strip me of everything I own, shut me up in prison, deprive me of all but the bare necessities to keep me alive, and still I'm free to make choices: what to think about, when to blink, whether to wiggle my little finger or my thumb. I could also make choices to paint my toenails red, marry the richest man in the world, and honeymoon on Neptune. But which of these choices could I fulfill in prison? Or even *not* in prison?

You see, I'm free to choose *anything*. The issue is: can I implement what I choose?

Growing up, becoming whole, fulfilling who we are and why we're here means seeking ways to expand the second part of freedom—the ability to implement our choices. This is the true path to growth for all life in the universe. God is God because he possesses perfect freedom to implement everything he chooses. Lucky for us, he's also pretty smart. With his perfect knowledge he is able to choose perfectly. Imagine absolute freedom in less than all-knowing hands. Even the tiniest shred of freedom is scary in the hands of an idiot.

Take me, for example.

The Parable of Joan:

Once upon a time, Joan lost 250 pounds.
This made Joan feel free, so she started up the path of life.
She got a job. She made money.
She bought her clothes in stores. Drove a car.
This was good. Joan was happy.
She liked being free and on the upward path.

But Joan wanted more freedom.
So she forged up the path and landed herself a better job.
Joan made better money.
She bought her clothes at Nordstrom. Drove a real nice car.
This was more good. Joan was even happier.
She was higher now on the path.

But Joan thought she wasn't high enough.
Joan wanted even more freedom.
She wanted to be at the top of the hill. NOW!
So Joan bought a house and got married.

But, oops! Poor Joan.
She took a detour.
Joan lost the freedom to fulfill her choices.
In fact, Joan almost got herself killed!

She did not go to the top of the hill, but to the bottom of the heap.

Joan wondered how to find the right path, again.
Joan wondered if she's even on the right hill.
Joan wondered if she ever knew a damned thing.

However, Joan was happy to be alive.
And she learned this lesson:

SHORTCUTS CAN BE TREACHEROUS.

PART FOUR

▼

THE WORLD'S BATTLEFIELDS HAVE BEEN IN THE HEART
CHIEFLY. . .

Henry Ward Beecher

DISCOVERED: FOOLPROOF FLAB REPELLENT

I was seventeen when I graduated from high school and moved out of The Big House. I couldn't muster a shred of regret over leaving home to go to college. If a family makes a house a home, then I'd been homeless since age eight because that's how long I'd been family-less.

I remember Momma calling the kids for Saturday morning housecleaning every week. Everybody had to get up and work, except me. At first, my brothers and sisters complained, "How come Joanie doesn't have to get up and help?" But Momma never assigned me any chores, and I took this as a sign that she didn't consider me a member of the family in good standing. Soon, everyone quit complaining and either tolerated me or grew indifferent.

Sometimes indifference frees a person. But I didn't feel free—I felt cast off. Many evenings in the schoolyard, I waited until dark to see if Momma would send someone to find me. No one ever came. My sisters got yelled at if they came home late, but never me. In my teens, I could leave on a Friday and not return until Monday, and nobody seemed to notice. So why should I regret leaving now, for good?

Truth was, I did hurt inside. I longed to be normal, accepted, and loved by my family. But on the day I moved out, no one offered me any sad good-byes. I pushed the hurt aside and walked away. Maybe I'd find acceptance in another town among people who didn't know I shouldn't be loved.

I had little contact with my family after that. Momma and I didn't speak to each other for two years. I enrolled at Solano Community College and found a job that, along with small student loans, would pay for tuition and living expenses. I'd gotten used to fending for myself as a child, so surviving in the real world came easily to me. Soon, life in The Big House had receded far from my thoughts. Being productive lessened the sense of shame I'd carried inside, and a new set of friends relieved the pain of long and lonely years. I still weighed almost 300 pounds, but maybe getting out on my own could change even that.

In two years, I earned my associate's degree in law enforcement and also my P.O.S.T. certificate, which stands for Police Officer Standards and Training. This certified me in firearms training, takedown and riot training, and other police intervention tactics. I was both the first African-American and the first woman to certify for P.O.S.T. at that college. This made me real proud.

After that, I moved to Sacramento and attended Sacramento State University to pursue a degree in criminal justice. There's not a lot to tell about my time at Sac State except to say that it came during the Viet Nam protest years. I'd given up the Peachee Wannabe look long ago; now the protest scene gave me a whole new way to dress: "militant" style. Militant was "in" on every college campus across America. Wanting to be "in," I cruised campus in black Frisco jeans, black T-shirt, army surplus jacket, and combat boots. Of course, it can be hard to look convincingly militant when you weigh 300 pounds, so I wore a militant attitude as a matching accessory. I strutted from class to class like some Ms-Black-Steamroller-Panther: "Just try messin' with me, you pro-establishment, anti-revolutionary capitalists, and I'll roll all over you!" In reality, I was still Jurassic Joan even though I was all grown up now and certified in firearms and lethal takedowns. Like a one-woman strike force, I was primed to defend myself with rotund dispatch!

But from what? And from whom? And why this desperation to avoid vulnerability at all costs? My memories of incest still hid behind the dark veil of denial. I acted militant but could never *be* militant. I had too much fear going on inside—too much even to protest the Viet Nam war properly.

Once, I got involved in a dangerous antiwar demonstra-tion—the takeover of a biology lab. Okay, so it wasn't *that* dangerous, but it was dissident, and in the early '70s, a little dis-sidence rounded out every college student's education. On the eve of the protest, I told the organizers, "Look guys, you need to know that I'm not sticking around for the actual takeover. I'll be the person who phones the TV and radio stations, but don't count on me for anything else." So, the next day, I called from a phone in another building and tipped off the media. Then I waited long enough for the news cameras to arrive and went home. I did *not* need dissidence badly enough to get myself arrested. From my law enforcement training, I *knew* what they did to people when they arrested them, and I did not want to be touched that way. It terrified me to be touched at all. In fact, during those days, if you came up from behind and threw your arms around me, I'd probably have thrown up right there.

Anyway, I didn't attend college to protest, but to graduate. Since high school, becoming a college graduate had been my only focus.

One day a bunch of students swarmed through the college buildings, shouting for everyone to leave their classes and join a boycott. This black guy busted in and yelled at me, "You, sister! You need to get out of here and join the boycott." I yelled back, "Listen, I paid tuition, honey—no way I'm leaving! *You* boycott if you want." And I didn't boycott. I stayed. My goal was clear—to get my degree—and I knew how to achieve it: attend classes, study, and keep a job to pay my way through. Anything more, I didn't bother with. Fewer choices make for a simpler life.

67
▼

And then one day, my persistence paid off. At the age of twenty-three—and Mrs. Weston's *stinky opinions* notwithstanding—I earned my bachelor's degree from Sacramento State University. And I earned it in spite of weighing 300 pounds, living below the poverty line, harboring emotional disorders, belonging to a disadvantaged race and gender, and enjoying *zero* family support through it all.

How did I accomplish this when before, my life had been so messed up? Easy. I let my passion to graduate have free reign over my life. And I'll tell you something: I gained almost *no weight* during my six years in college. I didn't resort to my usual pattern of mope and eat, mope and eat, because my passion to get a degree overpowered my pain. I felt joy and didn't need the false comfort that grazing at a bottomless buffet provided.

Great joy comes from satisfying one's inner passions. Passion inflames the heart with a sweet and intense longing. In turn, gratifying this longing brings sweet and intense pleasure—enduring pleasure, not the momentary high that comes from gratifying an addiction.

ADDICTION CONSUMES. PASSION FEEDS.

That seems ironic, but truth is often ironic. Certainly, satisfying my food addiction fed me, but it *fed* the part of me trying to maintain a lie. Maintaining lies consumes the energies of the spirit, making the inner voice difficult to hear. However, satisfying inner passions is—as they say—a whole *'nother* matter! More than mere physical desires, inner passions are deep-felt longings that generate vision and pull you in a direction of growth. They define you as unique because they are exclusively yours. By fulfilling your inner passions, you feed your spirit, build its strength, energize it. The inner voice grows strong, becomes almost audible, and listening for it attunes your ear. Your inner passions will always guide you toward becoming your truest, most productive self.

That's what pursuing a degree did for me. It magnified my truest self, and this gave me joy that overpowered pain and addiction.

The proof is in the pudding I didn't eat!

RARE IS THE BURDEN WHICH THE PURSUIT OF INNER
PASSION CAN'T RELIEVE.

SUN SCORCHED

Unfortunately, I had committed a near-fatal goof—but didn't know it. I had approached graduating from college without ever having considered what to do *after* I graduated. I'd kept my eyes on the prize but had become shortsighted in the process! Should I start a career? Get another degree? Emigrate to Bangladesh with the Peace Corps? Audition for Barnum and Bailey? Or what?

Having no passion to guide you is like demagnetizing the needle on a compass: it doesn't know which way to point.

That's how I felt after my graduation. No bearings.

Today, it's hard for me to believe that I never considered my postgraduation prospects. But remember, I never said, NOTHING SUPREMELY IDIOTIC AND TOTALLY LACKING IN FORESIGHT HAPPENS, EVER. It does. I proved it the day I donned another oversized cap and gown, received my certificate from the university president, and stepped off the podium without a parachute—of any color.

Bombs away, Joan Fountain!

I was about to experience a rough landing.

In my own behalf, I have to say I wasn't completely clueless; I knew I'd need to eat. So one summer day after the ceremonies, I went looking for a job—but only halfheartedly. I'd lost my passion for work since I wouldn't need to save for tuition. Besides, what work is suitable for a person weighing 300 pounds? Let's see . . . grape crusher . . . bridge-construction tester . . . ballast for an oil tanker, maybe. Law enforcement rejected me: no size 4X uniforms. I thought about trying elsewhere, but I hated the stunned looks I'd get when I asked people for job applications. And I dreaded those nosey little forms that always ask for your height and weight. There's only so far you can fudge on your weight, and I definitely fell outside the fudge factor. I could try fudging on my height to compensate, but nobody'd *ever* believe I was eight-foot, three!

But most dreadful was what happened the day a prospective employer first, examined my resume; second, noticed how my chair seat had been swallowed by my thighs; and third, said to me: "I'm sorry, Miss Fountain, we have no use for you at this time."

A normal person hears these words and feels disappointed. Me? I felt disposable, as if the woman had declared me a non-valid life form or something. You know how that feels? She might as well have pinned me to a plank and dissected my heart without the use of chloroform!

It was hot outside when I left her office, and I remember staggering to a bus stop where I sat for hours—those words ringing over and over in my head. *No use for you. No use for you.* The glaring sun and my own heavy emotions pressed me to the bench, and I felt glued there by sweat and despair. Buses slowed and opened their doors, but I couldn't stand up. The doors snapped shut, and bus after bus left me behind in a cloud of polluted thoughts. *We have no use for you.* With each missed ride, it seemed an old wound from childhood burst open inside me. I remembered my father's taunts, or Momma ignoring me during dinner, or cruel jokes my brothers pulled. *No use for you. I'm sorry.*

With no direction in life, no passion, a void had opened inside me, and the powerful emotions of my past swept easily in. I felt as I remembered feeling as a child: terribly wrong for this world and ashamed at something I didn't understand. Waves of pain surged through me in a riptide, pulling me under.

Buses arrived and buses left. The sun grew hotter, and the awful awareness burned in my head that getting a degree had been a wasted effort. The only self-worth I'd gained by it was false worth, and now even *that* began dripping off me like sweat, and my scam was revealed.

I started feeling exposed on that bench, as though I'd blown my cover and everyone could now confirm the truth: *we have no use for you.* I sensed people staring from passing cars and office-building windows, from the sidewalk across the street. I expected someone any moment to shout the alarm: "Look everyone, it's Joan Fountain! She's having an emotional meltdown right there on that public bench. Who told that girl she deserved *a life*, anyway?" Panic took over, and when the next bus pulled up, I couldn't get inside the door fast enough. I headed directly home, feeling as though I were running for cover the whole way. During the ride, I promised myself to quit looking for work. Society had no tolerance for nonentities like me.

I also promised myself to quit sitting on benches—especially on hot afternoons when I had nothing positive to think about.

Safe at home, I closed and locked the door. I decided not to go out in public anymore where people could accuse me of misappropriating a life. I felt guilty enough about it myself.

Fellow journey-takers, heed this advice:

BEARINGS. DON'T LEAVE HOME WITHOUT THEM.

71
▼

ON YOUR MARK . . .

The next morning, I didn't even get out of bed. Some people throw little pity parties when their emotions get them down. I do gala events. Since I'd had not just a bad day, but a bad *life*, I figured I deserved to stay home forever and celebrate. Of course, nobody else would get invited—I was an oversized party-of-one as it was. I convinced my roommate, Lynette, that I had some minor disease and would be staying home, and I waited for her to leave for work. Then, I got out of bed, drew the curtains, brought the phone in, and went back to bed— where I spent a few minutes reminding myself just how worthless I was. Then, having reached the proper level of self-pity for party throwing, I picked up the phone, put everything else in my life on hold, and ordered out!

Thus began my two-year eating binge that put Sleeping Beauty into a real coma. But no intravenous feeding for me, please. At *my* pity party, obtaining nourishment would never be so passive. I practiced the art of eating only in its rarest form: I elevated it to a sport!

On your mark . . .
Raise your fork(s) . . .
Stoke, baby stoke!

A talk show host once asked me what a person who weighs 420 pounds eats during a single meal.

"Give us an example, Joan," he said. "Tell the audience what you used to eat for breakfast."

"First," I said, "understand that when you have a severe food addiction, you don't eat breakfast."

"You don't?"

"No. You don't eat *meals*. You start eating when you get up in the morning, and you stop when you go to bed at night."

He laughed. "So every meal blends into the others."

"That's right. Of course, you eat breakfast foods in the morning and dinner foods in the evenings. So, to answer your question, in the mornings I used to eat a dozen eggs, a loaf of bread, a pound of bacon, a quarter-pound of butter, a pint of syrup—something like that."

The audience gasped on cue.

"Amazing. And for dinner?"

"A dutch oven full of spaghetti, or a turkey, or maybe a whole leg of lamb."

He winked at the camera. "With all the trimmings, I suppose."

"Of course! And then I'd top it off with a half-gallon of ice cream."

"The whole container?"

"The whole container—and I'd finish it before it had a chance to *melt*, mind you."

The audience laughed and applauded. They wouldn't have if they had ever caught sight of me slumped across the couch cushions, one hand holding the ice cream, the other working a serving spoon rapidly between carton and mouth. Not too laughable—especially realizing that, while eating, my eyes never leave the late-late show blaring on the TV in front of me. I'm not even aware of that ice cream. My feed-arm is on automatic. I stuff the frozen goo past my lips and let it dribble down my throat, but I never taste it, never enjoy it. Like *breathing*, I did it so often, why *care* about it?

Most times, though, I *did* care. A delicious meal—all my favorite foods spread from table edge to table edge—could make me care a lot! The sight and smell of all that food, loading it onto my plate, the texture of it in my mouth, the sensation of swallowing. A meal could become the center of my universe for hours. I'd hunker over it in a trance, surround it with my arms and my face, pull it symbolically into me like communion. Of course, every bite mounded layers of fat onto my body and around every precious internal organ. I knew I was killing myself with each forkful. And yet, it would have killed me to leave leftovers.

Now, how do you explain *that* to a television audience?

I couldn't explain it even to myself. Couldn't explain that I sensed the child in me, Joanie, demanding to be fed. That I couldn't let her starve because her job was critical to my survival. She held a dark and terrifying secret in that dreaming-place of hers. She'd reveal it if I didn't keep her fat and happy.

And if I died, who'd give a care? Not even Momma, I bet. She had lost track of Joanie long ago and had never really introduced herself to *Joan*. My life was my own to keep or to lose. I considered it nobody's business if I ate ice cream by the container or if I broke the Oreo Law by downing them too quickly to pull them apart first or if I tied Lays packages to my face and used them as feedbags. I was in training for the Olympics, and these methods helped me perfect my serve.

"You seem, Joan," the TV host said, "to be the sort of person

74
▼

who—when you decide to do something—you do it all the way."

"Yes, I am," I answered. "There's no halfway with me. When I go for something, I go all the way."

"And when you give up . . . ?"

"I give up all the way, too."

"You wanted to die."

"No." I paused. "But I didn't want to live either. I couldn't use pills or a gun or a high bridge—they're too much like suicide, and I don't believe in that. I overate because it kept me between living and dying. It was the perfect weapon. I could nourish myself and kill myself at the same time."

"That's sad," he said.

"It's very sad," I said, and I sensed the camera lens close in on my face. "Addiction is a sign of despair. It was the saddest, loneliest, darkest time of my life. I never want to experience it again."

75
▼

YOU CANNOT BE DESTROYING YOURSELF IN ANY WAY, CONSCIOUSLY OR UNCONSCIOUSLY, AND BE HAPPY.

THE MOST UNNATURAL ACT OF ALL

Whenever I stare into the night sky, I'm amazed at the miracle of our universe. Billions of galaxies exist out there, each with its own system of stars and planets. But there's a whole lot of emptiness out there, too—light-centuries of emptiness. Space is nothing but a big black void with floaties. Scientists speculate about the presence of life on some of those floaties, but nobody speculates whether life exists in the immense vacuum between them. My momma used to suck up live moths with her Eureka upright, but that's not what we're talking about here. You've seen astronauts wearing those incredible million-dollar suits to protect them during space walks. They'd die in a moth's heartbeat without them. The vacuum of space would suck their lungs inside out, not to mention the other unpleasant effects of depressurization. Believe me, the big black void is not our friend.

That's why I am awestruck by the miracle of Earth. Surrounded by the deadly emptiness of space, Earth is a life raft.

It comes equipped with all the chemical building blocks of organic life as well as the right atmospheric conditions for life to sustain itself. Our Creator has finely tuned every aspect of our natural world for two purposes: the replenishing and the nurturing of life, the firstborn child of love.

IN GOD VERSUS THE GREAT VOID, LIFE ALWAYS WINS.

In such a life-affirming world then, the useless destruction of life must be the most unnatural act of all. Realizing this, today, I regret trying to destroy myself. However, The Creator is over all. He knows what burdens pressed upon my heart. For two years I begged Him to swallow me up into that void where nothing exists. But He kept saying no. So, while it was painful to live and painful not to be able to end my life, worse yet was the pain in knowing that even The Big Guy had turned His back on me. There was only one thing I could do: dial out for a double pepperoni with extra cheese and try God again later.

The problem was, Little Caesar's wouldn't donate to the cause. I survived for a while on unemployment checks and my roommate's generosity, but as my body expanded, so did my appetite. To her credit, Lynette tried to support me as much as she could. Situations in her own life had made her an outcast like me, and she wouldn't abandon me. But she and I had this habit of mine to feed, and we couldn't do it alone. Lynette had to get me on welfare.

But over the next year, I grew fatter and fatter, like a grotesquely swelling slug. By the time I reached 375 pounds, I could barely maneuver myself from room to room. To get an idea of what it was like, imagine being imprisoned in at least twenty layers of thick winter coats and you have to try to do

77
▼

everything with them on because they are part of you. Live like that every day and night, shambling from bedroom to bathroom to kitchen back to bedroom. It's a prisoner's life, only you never leave your cell. You carry it with you wherever you go. And you feel rotten. High blood pressure. Edema. Every joint swells and hurts when you move. It's a labor just to breathe. All your extremities tank up with fluids, making big old fat sausages of your fingers and toes.

But these symptoms appeared gradually. I didn't get up one morning to the shock of my huge image in the mirror and say, "Oh, look what happened to me during the night. I gained 200 pounds! Darn it all" No. My conditions crept up on me, allowing me time to adjust. One night I noticed that putting an extra pillow under my shoulders helped me to breathe easier. Several months later, I added another and shifted my body toward the head of the bed where the wall added support to the pillows. Before long, I was sleeping completely sitting up. This position seemed natural to me. I sat all day and sat all night. I seldom left my bed anymore.

THE MOST DANGEROUS TRANSFORMATIONS ARE THOSE WHICH STEAL IN SLOWLY UNTIL THE THINGS YOU VALUE MOST ARE SUDDENLY AT RISK.

Before I knew it, I'd developed a habit that consumed $100 a day in groceries. Welfare benefits were not enough; we had to find additional aid. Lynette came home one day with some news.

"I asked some people at work," she said, "and I think you might qualify for SSI and SSP."

"What's SSI and SSP?" I asked.

"State and social security programs. They pay pretty well, but you'll have to be interviewed and tested to qualify."

"Tested?"

"Yeah. Psychological tests and some physical, but . . . "

I finished for her, "But physically my problems are obvious enough to qualify me."

"Probably."

"So they'll send over a shrink to find out if I sucked my fists as a child or if I ever got chased by a pack of fat, ravenous dogs."

"I don't know," she laughed, "but they need to see you're not faking it. Some people fake disabilities because these programs pay so well."

A few weeks later, a social worker came to the house and discovered that I wasn't faking my weight problem. This woman was rather skinny and I don't suppose she was faking her weight problem, either. She asked me a few questions, and my answers show just how bizarre my thinking was back then:

SW: How do feel about your life, Joan.

JF: My life is good. Really good. I'm so happy, really. I graduated from college a year and a half ago, you know.

SW: Yes, I read that on your application. Congratulations.

JF: Thanks very much. I had several job options, but I'm continuing my education at home instead. Here, look at these books I'm reading. This one is on the Inuit, and this one, the Chinese. I have a really interesting one on African ritual.

SW: Nice.

JF: World cultures fascinate me. Now that I've chosen not to work, I have plenty of time to study them.

SW: Joan, may I ask: do you experience any pain—I mean, stemming from your condition?

JF: I'm sure I do, but you know, I'm in control of it pretty well. Really. You'd hardly know.

SW: Tell me about your family life—growing up.

JF: My family life? Oh, it was great. My family . . . I mean, we were exactly like the Brady Bunch. You know what I'm saying? Exactly. Happy, happy, happy, happy. Like the Brady Bunch.

SW: And today—you still get along?

JF: Like the Brady Bunch. Happy all the time. Yep. I could have been a black Brady sister! Exactly.

See? I warned you I had gotten a little goofy. *The Brady Bunch?* Might as well compare the Manson family to the Cleavers. (Sorry.) But I said it to her without even blinking. People in denial are good liars—even to themselves. They have to be in order to recruit enablers—people they can manipulate into lending support. I myself actually believed my father could have been Mike Brady!

Wishful thinking, maybe. Mike would never have taken on a black mistress.

Anyway, I successfully bamboozled this social worker—not that I really needed to. I was legitimately disabled, physically. A short time after her visit, I received a document from the State of California certifying me as permanently disabled and qualifying me for government assistance. The state would cover my food bill for as long as I lived—which might not be long, since the government was now helping me kill myself. God had refused to be my ultimate enabler, but I'd enlisted a whole slew of practicing enablers for stand-ins: thirty million Californians.

IN GOD VERSUS CALIFORNIA, THE GREAT VOID ALWAYS WINS.

ROT, ROT, ROT TILL THE BROAD DAYLIGHT

Four hundred pounds—and the months passed in weeks; weeks in days; days in hours, then minutes. Time developed stretch marks as I waited to die. The house grew cramped, and I retired permanently to bed. On the floor near the bed sat bags of groceries and teetering stacks of books, creating a bedside library-cafe. All my favorite foods and books within arm's reach and available around the clock. What more could I want? I gave a new meaning to the term "voracious reader."

But high blood pressure began damaging my eyes. First, the corners of my room became filled with shadows. Then the shadows spread, making me the center of a shrinking sphere of light. Soon, I would not be able to read, and the only activities left to me would be eating and sleeping.

But sometimes I felt too tired even to eat—my arms too heavy to lift my food. My poor old heart had to pump double time to force blood through all those layers of fat. Why it continued to beat at all, I don't know. Couldn't it sense the inevitable? I felt not just tired, but battle weary and spiritless. The weight of my body had now grown equal with the weight of my shame, and I wanted release from both.

When my kidneys started to fail, Lynette tried to get me to see a doctor, but I refused to leave the house.

"Joan," she pleaded, "this is serious."

"I can't, Lynette," I said. "We can't afford to pay a doctor."

"SSI and SSP will pay."

"I'll be fine." I said. "I'll rest up and get better. I'm not ready to go out, and don't ask me to."

"Rest up? All you do is sit in that bed and *rot* around the clock."

We laughed and sang the song, using Lynette's revised wording, "One o'clock, two o'clock, three o'clock, rot! . . . " and it did feel good to laugh. But, of course, she was right—I'd never get better. We ended our duet and grew silent.

Lynette looked at me. "What are you going to do?"

"I don't know," I answered. "But whatever it is, you're going to have to do it for me."

"I do everything for you," she said.

"And don't you forget it, girl," I smiled.

One morning, several weeks later, I woke up to find blood seeping from between my legs—and it wasn't time for my period. Blood flowed steadily through the morning, and at noon, I phoned Lynette at work.

"Joan," she said, "get ready. I'm going to borrow a car and take you to the hospital." She hung up before I could say no.

An hour later, wearing the only dress that fit me—the polka-dot dress you've seen in my picture—I trundled toward the open front door where Lynette waited to drive me to the emergency room. I felt foggy-headed from the loss of blood. The sting from the sun through the doorway irritated my eyes like a foreign object. It had been two years since I last stepped through that doorway and into the spotlight of the sun. What made me think I had the courage to do it now? But Lynette had gone through the hassle of borrowing a car, and she was standing there waiting to help. I felt dizzy and suddenly couldn't remember why I'd come home two years earlier and locked myself up.

Lynette saw me falter and came to me. "Can you make it?" she said, lifting my arm across her shoulder to support me.

"No. You'll have to make it for me."

"I always do."

We shuffled toward the door.

"Well, girl," I said, "don't expect me to be grateful."

And, heart pounding triple time, I closed my eyes against the light and let her guide me out to the waiting car.

83

▼

A FRIEND IS MORE THAN A FRIEND WHEN SHE BUILDS A BRIDGE FROM THE DARK INTO THE LIGHT.

PART FIVE

▼

I knew that if God loved me then I could do
wonderful things ... For what could stand
against me with God, since one person, any person, with God constitutes the majority?

That knowledge humbles me, melts my bones,
closes my ears, and makes my teeth rock loose-
ly in their gums. And it also liberates me ...

Maya Angelou

BYPASS

The diagnosis was Morbid Obesity, a term that groups together all the symptoms of obesity and says you'll probably die from one or more of them soon. In my case, my doctor, Doc Lowell, said I had six months to live.

"Unless," Doc Lowell said, "you agree to a surgical procedure called an intestinal bypass that will cause you to lose weight and may possibly save your life."

"May possibly?" I asked.

"Nothing is certain. But if you agree to the surgery, we'll need time to prepare."

"For what?"

"Miss Fountain," the doc checked his clipboard, "your weight is four hundred and twenty pounds. We'll need to build a special surgical platform for you. This hospital is not equipped with surgical tables large enough for a person such as yourself. It would be a first here."

So, if I agreed to this surgery, I would be not only the first African-American woman to certify in firearms and takedowns at Solano Community College but also the fattest person they ever operated on at Oakland's Kaiser Hospital. At this rate I was racking up more impressive accomplishments than Imelda Marcos.

"Do it," I said. But I said it without enthusiasm because I wasn't sure I wanted him to save my life.

"Then we'll order the platform. But I feel obligated to warn you that the extent of your obesity complicates this procedure, as it would any surgical procedure. You may not live through it."

"That wouldn't matter to me, Doc," I said. "I haven't really been living for the past couple of years, anyway."

So, I signed the forms, returned home, and waited two weeks while the hospital constructed a platform sturdy enough to allow Doc Lowell to cut me open and tinker with my intestines and not fall to pieces (the platform, not the doctor). I decided to inform my mother about this (the tinkering, not the platform), so, late one night, I dialed her number.

"Momma, it's Joan," I said when she answered.

"Hello, Joanie." Her voice sounded distant, as if she were holding the phone at arm's length from her mouth.

"Momma, can you hear me?"

"Of course I can hear."

"I'm really sick, Momma. I'm going to have an operation. I thought I'd let you know."

"What kind of operation?"

"An intestinal bypass. They . . ."

"When."

"Next Thursday, but listen, you don't need to come, Momma, if . . ."

"I'll be sure and pray for you, Joanie. On Thursday."

"Okay, pray for me and . . . thank you. . . ."

I listened for a response. I couldn't even hear her breathing.

"I'll call and let you know how it turns out."

I didn't put the phone down after we said good-bye—there

was more I wanted to say. But I didn't know what I wanted Momma to hear, so when the line went dead, I felt relieved. At the same time, a hollow longing settled into my heart. I wanted to cry, but I couldn't.

A while later, I fell asleep—the phone still in my lap.

BYPASS: A PROCEDURE IN WHICH A DISEASED ORGAN IS TEMPORARILY OR PERMANENTLY CIRCUMVENTED (SEE WEBSTER'S).

CARRIED AWAY

Thursday came, and at dawn, Lynette and I began our drive to Oakland. I'd had two weeks to consider my feelings about the operation and was surprised that morning to feel hope rising with the sun. I'd come to believe that obesity had been the cause of my troubles all along and that if surgery could make me thin forever, I might finally be happy.

At the hospital, Lynette helped me through admittance; then an orderly wearing a white baseball cap brought a wheel-chair to take me to my room. He quickly realized that no way was I going to squeeze my butt into that chair, and he spun around and disappeared back down the hall. He returned a minute later pushing a steel gurney with sturdy looking wheels. The contraption wasn't wide enough for me to lie on, but rid-ing sidesaddle in the middle of it might work.

"This should do it, Miss," he said and cranked a handle that lowered the bed. He maneuvered the gurney behind me, and I plopped down. The braces squeaked, but they held. The orderly didn't attempt to crank the bed back up, but he said with a cheery smile, "You see?"

Lynette hugged me. "You're on your own from here," she said.

"Go ahead. Abandon me," I replied.

"No one deserves it more." She smiled and then waved as the orderly wheeled me off—my sandals dragging across the tiled floor.

For the next few hours, I sat half-on, half-off a hospital bed that threatened any moment to collapse while two nurses prepped me for the operation. They washed me, took blood samples, and measured my vital signs. By Doc Lowell's orders, the nurses refused to feed me—in fact they had to administer three enemas to eliminate what I'd eaten the day before! It was humiliating. I got through it only by reminding myself repeatedly how great I'd look a year from then with a body like Goldie Hawn's on *Laugh-In*. In fact, I thought, this entire scene belongs on *Laugh-In*, and I double-checked the room for hidden cameras.

At noon, I gazed longingly at the lunch belonging to the woman in the bed next to mine. It was a meager snack really: a cheese sandwich, applesauce, and a cookie, but I would have eagerly endured another enema for it.

A male nurse came in with orders to insert two IVs—one on top of my wrist and one under my clavicle. First, he tried to find a vein through all the flab on my wrist, but his failure to do so was not due to a dull needle. Poke and miss, poke and miss—and he cussed at every miss. Finally, he gave up and called for the nurses to assist. With efforts from all three, they cut a slit in my arm which reached two-inches in length before they hit a vein large enough to make blood squirt across the bed and onto the wall. They stuck the IV in that hole and taped it shut. They tried the same trick with my clavicle but couldn't make my blood spurt far enough. They ended up sticking the IV under my collarbone instead. I was a bloody wreck by the time the anesthesiologist showed up.

"Hi, Joan," she said. "My name's Dr. Yee, and I'm going to give you a sedative to knock you out for the operation."

"Too late," I said. "They've already operated."

She laughed and prepared her rather long needle. "This won't take effect immediately," she said, and I felt a sting in my thigh. "We don't want you falling asleep until we've got you positioned in the hoist."

"Positioned in what hoist?" I said.

"The industrial hoist Dr. Lowell ordered. We would never get you onto the surgical platform without a hoist." She jerked out the needle and patted my thigh.

Hoist, I thought. Did she mean crane? Great. They'd hired a crane to come in and lift me onto the table—probably operated by some guy named Mack with hairy arms and a beer-stained tank top.

I hope this sedative is strong, I thought. I don't want to be sober for this.

The orderly in the white baseball cap showed up smiling at the door. "You ready, Dr. Yee? I've brought the gurney."

"Yes, Mack," she answered, and my eyebrows shot up. "Let's take her down."

A few minutes later, Mack wheeled me into the operating room, and Doc Lowell and his assistants slapped electrodes onto my bleeding body. Then they helped me to maneuver myself onto a wide platform suspended by metal cables. A hoist would lift this platform with me lying on it, carry it to the center of the room, and bring it to rest atop a receiving platform which sat solidly on eight sturdy legs.

However, as it turned out, the hoist would carry me farther than that. Much farther. Just as I got seated on the platform,

Dr. Yee's sedative suddenly took effect, and I went limp. I fell backwards, landing solidly on my back in the middle of the platform. My vision faded to black.

Fortunately, I had fallen into perfect position for the operation. Unfortunately, by the time the hoist carried me across to the receiving platform, I had died, and the room erupted with alarms.

THE GRAND KEY

It had been nearly two years since I last laid flat—a detail I had forgotten to tell Doc Lowell. Now, my large chest pressed heavily on my lungs and heart. They couldn't sustain the weight. I flat-lined (so to speak) as I smothered beneath the bulk of my own fat. I'm told that Doc Lowell's team snapped into action and within minutes resuscitated me, then proceeded with the operation. But, of course, I wasn't aware of any of this. I experienced something the surgical team was unaware of and which—to this day—I can't adequately describe.

Most of us have become acquainted with the term "near-death experience," and I suppose that's what I had. I saw no tunnel, no bright light or angelic beings—I just fell backwards and landed into a soft, black void rather than onto the hard surface of the platform. Normally with a fall, I would have tried to catch myself because even fat people have reflexes. Sensing I no longer had a body that could get hurt, I just went along for the ride. And what a ride! I'll tell you, you never feel so good as when you're dead. I wanted to let out an infinite sigh of relief. Every pain had disappeared. All my hunger and self-doubt were simply gone. I was a being of spirit. I felt wholly myself—my natural and true self. I was in my prime. I don't mean to brag, but in the spirit, I possessed a truly celestial physique! I showed no trace of my tubby tummy, thunder thighs, or beluga butt.

Jenny Craig, you should know, girl, you'll need a new job when you get to heaven.

Not that I believed I was in heaven or anything. But when I looked around me, a billion-billion stars blinked on, and heaven seemed close enough to touch. I shifted my body and flew to the blackness beyond the stars and then turned to catch the view. And what a Kodak moment! The entire universe— our beautiful, abundant universe—spread before my eyes in an immense, white-fired sphere.

But more than my eyes took in this sphere—all my senses took it in, as well as my awareness. My spirit drew the universe inside of me, or the universe drew me inside of it. However it happened, I *knew* all of creation from every perspective at once—top to bottom, side to side, outside to inside. I knew the broad reaches of the galaxies, and at the same time, I knew the hidden hearts of the tiniest particles.

With this view, I understood at once the order of the universe. Its composition, dynamics, and rhythms of operation became clear. I saw that, as The Creator's handiwork, our universe is vast and grand but also simple and obvious and sublime. I grasped this key to its mysteries:

WE ARE ALL THE BIG US—MIRACULOUSLY CREATED, INSEPARABLY CONNECTED.

I didn't have long to consider this. The instant it occurred to me, whump! I fell back into my body. Just like that—whump!— as if my mortal body carried a pull of gravity too strong for my spirit to resist any longer. It was like Dorothy's house crashing to the ground in the Land of Oz—unceremonious and sudden. My body still slept under the effect of anesthetics, but my spirit remained aware for a moment. The surgical room lights glared white hot. Tubes ran down my throat. Two of Doc Lowell's team supported my leg in the air while a third wrapped it with ace bandages. "Hurry that up," the doc said to them. "I'd like to get started here." Then I blanked out.

Later, when I slid open my eyes, an oxygen mask rested over my nose and mouth. I lay in a double-wide bed—or maybe two beds pushed together with the heads raised so I could breathe. Doc Lowell was standing nearby.

"Hi, Joan," he said. "We're going to keep you here in the recovery room through the night. Everything went fine with the operation, except that we lost you for a minute before we got started."

"You loshed me?" My lips were like lead.

"Yes, but we got you back. You're a strong woman."

"You shaid to hurry wish my legsh."

"You were out cold—how did you hear that?"

"The bandagesh . . ."

"To prevent blood clots. You get some sleep, now. I'll check back later."

He crossed the room, passing five other recovering patients, and walked out the door. I didn't call him back to describe what happened from my perspective when I'd "died." He would probably call it hallucinating, and I didn't know how to argue with that. It was reality, and I shouldn't have to defend it to anyone. Besides, though I had become one with the entire universe, I didn't feel that the experience was meant to be universal. It felt private. Just me and the universe. Until I knew what good purpose sharing it would serve, I decided to keep what I experienced to myself.

But I had other things to think about. The surgery was behind me, and realizing that my body would now absorb only a portion of what I ate made me smile under my mask. I closed my eyes and tried to count all the ways my life would change. I got to sixty-three before I fell asleep.

Sometime in the night, I woke up when a nurse in blue entered the room. She moved from patient to patient, checking each one's condition and jotting down numbers from electronic monitors that beeped and hummed near every bed. She worked through the room purposefully, and yet this nurse was not just making her rounds. She spent an extra minute at each bedside to arrange the blankets of those who slept, dim the lamps, review each patient's face. She made personal, caring contact with each one, and the words "We are all the BIG US" came to my mind.

She arrived at my bed, and after updating my chart and checking the fluid in my IVs, she tucked the blankets in along the side of my mattress. Her hair—black, streaked with gray— was tied back with a wide, white ribbon. I wondered about the mirror, the bathroom, the house where she had tied that ribbon on. I wanted to know her, everything about her.

"Are you comfortable?" she asked.

I nodded.

Then she rested her hand on my shoulder, and through her touch, I felt compassion flow. "Rest easy," she said and moved on to the next bed.

Words from the past rang out in my head: *no use for you.* But this time I dared to shout back, *Who* has no use for me? Not Lynette or this nurse—*they* have use for me. They care. Even my gurney-driver, Mack—he's kind to me and doesn't judge me for my problems. So there's three people, at least, with use for me in their lives. Not to mention The Creator, who must have *some* use for me. Why else would He make me one with the universe and then let me live to remember it?

What a concept. *The Creator* had use for me!

I snuggled into the warmth of my blankets to relish the feeling, and waves of wonder washed through me. They rivaled even the thrill that one day I might become Goldie Hawn's black twin!

See what caring and kindness lead to? The Creator uses the touch of others to let us feel His touch. The nurse in the white ribbon helped to heal more than just my body that night in the recovery room. Her caring showed that she already knew The Grand Key to the natural universe. He touch reclaimed me as part of of the BIG US.

I mentioned that my reentry into my body was like Dorothy's house landing in Oz—but the analogy doesn't end there. Compared to the world beyond, Earth can seem as unreal and disorienting as Dorothy found Oz to be. This is not our natural home. It would be nice to just click our heels together and go to our real home where *nothing* impedes growth and joy. However, I've learned that there are good reasons for having no easy outs. We must progress *here* while we're here and—like Dorothy's friends—acquire hearts that love, brains equipped with wisdom and truth, and courage to find and follow our yellow-brick roads. By gaining any measure of these, we grow. But to gain the full measure, we must lend our strength to others. Remember The Way of the Universe: life nurtures life. Creation must nurture creation, or everything reverts to chaos.

So, no matter how far on this journey we think we've come, it's never ours to say we've come far enough. Only God can make that call. Like the Tin Man, the Scarecrow, and the Lion, we don't own magic slippers that can end our journey by a click of the heels. This is because we're meant to learn and then to stay behind, to link arms and help others along the road.

LOVING IS THE MOST NATURAL ACT OF ALL.

THE CLUE IN THE VOID

I prayed for God to swallow me into the void, and he did that day in surgery. But He pulled a fast one and brought me back. Now I've got Him figured. When He says no, He actually means yes—but yes to something far finer than what we know to ask for.

It's like praying to tour the neighborhood on a new pair of roller blades, and The Creator says no because what He's got in mind for you is a flight on the space shuttle. Talk about touring the 'hood! Your lips will never flap again about not getting that pair of skates.

WITH GOD IN THE BARGAIN, NEVER DOUBT YOU GOT THE BETTER DEAL.

Let me give you some advice. When you pray to The Creator, pray this: "Okay, I admit it, I'm clueless and you're The Clue. So let Your will be done. Not mine." Believe me, you'll be better off for it. You and I are creators, too—capable of creating lots of good or ill by our own efforts. We produce wonderful, joyful creations when we persist in things that make our spirits thrive. On the other hand, we cause pain by our creations which conflict with the natural tendencies of the spirit. Either way, the Master Creator honors our efforts. It would break natural law for him not to. So:

BE CAREFUL WHAT YOU PERSIST IN—YOU'LL PROBABLY GET IT.

Luckily, this is a universe of wake-up calls. Disaster always comes with warnings. But sometimes, out of pride or fear, we charge bullheadedly down destructive paths anyway. And when we do, The Creator doesn't step in to save our behinds. Consequences are sacred. Without them, how would we ever learn?

So far, in my story, I'm a slow learner. I had the bad habit of coming up with my own twisted solutions for my troubles. These included: Fattening up in order to protect myself. Depending on a college degree to hand me success in life. Acquiring a husband to feel complete. Hiding from life to avoid dealing with its realities. Praying to die as a release from the pain of living. No wonder I lay in recovery after emergency surgery to save my life! Going under the knife was just the natural consequence of my choices. I deserved it. In fact I *chose* it by denying or misunderstanding all the earlier consequences that came as warning signs of disaster.

Some wise person has said that humanity's solutions to humanity's problems are like rearranging deck chairs on the *Titanic*. Don't I know it! Put me alone behind the captain's wheel, and my ship will go down every time. It's only when I invite The Creator—the Master Seaman—to stand behind me and whisper in my ear that I make it safely into the harbor.

I used to believe that nothing existed in the void between

the stars. I was wrong. For one thing, scientists have discovered something there they call "antimatter." (It was probably *me* they detected.) But scientists will never discover such a thing as "anti*life*" because The Creator is life, and His gentle, life-sustaining influence is everywhere—even in the void. I know. I was there. And I'm convinced that the only perfect use of our lives is to bring about The Creator's will. It makes *natural* sense, doesn't it? I mean, after all:

HE IS IN CHARGE.

GETTING TO "DUH!"

Mistakes can be our best teachers. Some of us, though, have to repeat our mistakes over and over before we finally get things right. And when we do, we say, "duh!" because what's right is always present—and therefore obvious when we finally see it.

The object of life is getting to "duh!" as quickly and as painlessly as possible. But there's a catch: the short course to "duh!" is seldom the safe course. The Creator never leads us to "duh!" through unnatural shortcuts. We forge them for ourselves.

Could this be a clue? Are we meant to take the *long* road to the top when it's the safe road? Can our struggles sometimes tell us that we're on the right path? I say yes, yes, yes! I say that struggling isn't always BAD and that *getting* to "duh!" as opposed to *arriving* there has its own joyous rewards.

Wishing to circumvent the *process* of life is a death wish—believe me, I know. Take Mom Nature for example. She doesn't hurry or take shortcuts. She adapts naturally to her circumstances by taking her time and by making minute self-adjustments as she goes. The Galapagos turtles couldn't change the unfriendly nature of their new island home, so they changed their own nature to suit it. They *evolved* in the face of challenge. To have stubbornly refused either the truth of their predicament or the rigors of change would have made them extinct.

People and turtles belong to the same natural world. When people resist the natural process of growth, or try to circumvent it, they mutate in unnatural ways and run the risk of extinction, the surgeon's table, or lifelong addictions which rob them of freedom, the ability to grow, and the capacity for joy.

Struggling to learn the truth about ourselves is productive. Struggling against the truth about ourselves is not. If we can learn from turtles, we can also learn from trees: When the wind of truth blows, it's best to bend with it like the willow than to resist it and break like the oak.

THE SWAY OF TRUTH IS IRRESISTIBLE. NOTHING IN NATURE CAN RESIST IT OR TRY TO AVOID IT, AND EXPECT TO THRIVE.

103

▼

We'll never get to "duh!" by being rigid. We'll just cycle through the same mistakes over and over. Recycling our trash is good. Recycling our mistakes is not. The best advice I can give to avoid repeating our mistakes is this: Check in with The Big Guy on occasion. Use whatever method works for you, but do it. You know you can trust His advice because He's already gotten THE BIG "DUH!" Respect that. Let Him know He's everything to you and that you invite and appreciate His clueing you in now and then.

Beyond this, here are ten suggestions that make getting to "duh!" quicker and less painful.

1. Seek the balance and perspective that religion and spirituality offer.

2. Adopt a set of moral standards and priorities by which to judge your actions and choices. Never compromise your standards, and only compromise your priorities if it would serve the overall good to do so.

3. Learn to recognize the inner signals of your spirit that tell you when you're on or off course.

4. Have courage to correct your course whenever needed and at whatever cost.

5. Stay away from people and influences that tend to pull you off course.

6. Be humble. Never assume you're right about anything; rather, always be willing to learn.

7. Step out of your usual thought patterns by keeping yourself open to new or even surprising ideas—but ideas which complement what you already know to be true.

8. Once you recognize truth, hold firmly to it, regardless of your own feelings or those of others. What we *feel* does not always coincide with what we *know* to be right for ourselves.

9. Take responsibility for your actions and whatever consequences they bring. You can't learn from choices you don't acknowledge as your own.

10. Keep in mind that all things in the universe, especially your own unique experiences, are designed to help you grow.

PART SIX

▼

In order to be a realist, you must believe in miracles.

David Ben Gurion

STRAIGHT FLUSH

Aweek after my surgery, Doc Lowell gave me the high sign, and Lynette drove me home. I noticed right away the effects of surgery on my digestive track. I could eat as much food as I wanted, but little of it stayed with me—but that's putting it delicately. Truth was, surgery turned me into a walking enema, and if I spent half my time eating, you can guess how I spent the other half. Lynette noticed a rise in the water bill from all that flushing, but I just looked at her and shrugged. "What do you expect me to do?" I said. "Visit the neighbors?"

"It would help," she replied.

We bought new bathroom scales, and every day, it marked a weight loss. The fat just melted off! I swear I could just stand still on the scales and see the needle edge slowly down the dial like the hand of a backwards clock. Doc Lowell's magic knife had worked. What took years to put on took months to come off.

But the surgery altered more than just my colon. My sour mood melted away as fast as my flab. I started keeping the house cleaner. I liked the curtains drawn open instead of closed. I could walk easier, breathe easier. With more oxygen flow, my thoughts seemed clearer, more positive. As my body lightened, so did my despair. Soon I ventured outside to pull weeds and to look at flowers. Even the dandelions in the grass struck me as beautiful. I walked to the corner and back, and NOTHING BAD HAPPENED. No one assaulted me or told me to get on home where people like me belonged. I made trips to the neighborhood market, and then felt comfortable taking the bus to the grocery story, the library, and to the homes of old college friends. I had buried myself deep but was resurfacing again, and it felt good.

When a year passed, a remarkable thing had occurred. I phoned Momma to give her the news.

"Momma, I've lost 100 pounds!"

"That's good."

"I wanted to tell you," I said, "that I think your prayers helped. God must listen to you."

107

▼

"I listen to *Him*, Joan," she said.

"Lynette's trying to talk me into to goin' *dancing* tonight to celebrate. Can't you see me, Momma, shimmying around?"

"You enjoy yourself, and call me again sometime."

"Okay, Momma."

She hung up, and I said into the dead phone, "You're way too excitable, Momma. I really think you should get control of your enthusiasm." I dropped the phone onto the cradle.

That night we *did* go dancing and had a wonderful, crazy time. I even wore a new dress I'd recently made for myself. Can you imagine a 320-pound woman disco dancing across the floor to BeeGees tunes? I must have reminded folks of one of those pink ballerina hippos in Walt Disney's *Fantasia*. I didn't care—let people snicker. A year before, I'd hardly been able to get out of bed. Now, I was hot-shoeing it around, whipping up my own Thursday Night Fever. I felt unembarrassed—even giddy.

Grooving to the music made all my sorrows beat a retreat, and I was elated.

But my Thursday Night Fever was a short-lived fantasia. A few months passed, and I lost another twenty pounds or more, but then one day I stepped onto the scales, and my knees almost buckled at the results.

I had gained—not lost—two pounds.

I flew to the phone.

"Doc Lowell," I said, "something's terribly wrong, here."

"What's that, Joan."

"I've *gained* two pounds."

"Joan, that's normal."

"But I prefer the other normal!"

He made an appointment for me to see him, and a few days later I sat across from him in his office.

"It's been over a year since we operated," the doc was saying. "Your metabolism is finally balancing with your body's lower food-absorption rate. We expected this to happen."

"*I* didn't," I said. "I thought I bought a one-way ticket to skinny, not a round-trip."

"Then you'll have to reduce your food intake. Continue eating as you are, and you'll just gain weight."

No! No! No! I wasn't supposed to have to *work* to get thin—the surgery was supposed to make it automatic.

The doc continued, "I'll recommend a diet plan, and if you stick with it you should be fine. Give it a try, and see me in six months or so."

I left the doc's office absolutely dejected. I rode the bus home and went straight to bed. I'd never be able to *diet*. Even the sound of the word made me shudder. Diet was only one letter away from *die* and, if you asked me, less desirable. Dieting was for regular people, and I didn't want to be *regular*. All my life I'd wanted to be regular until I started losing weight. Then, shedding 150 pounds made me *better* than regular for once, put me a cut above instead of below. "You're looking sooooo *good*," friends would squeal. "How do you do it, girl?" Of course I never told. I needed to be special, needed to have my own secrets for success. I even started fantasizing that it was willpower making me loose weight instead of Doc Lowell's version of cut-and-paste.

Khh! Flush *that* fantasy down the toilet. My previous year seemed like a sham, now that I'd have to fight the flab the hard way. From here on, it was *diet* or *die*.

How I loathed reality.

109

▼

FANTASIES ARE FOES DISGUISED AS FRIENDS. ENTERTAIN
THEM AS BRIEFLY AS POSSIBLE, AND NEVER GIVE THEM
YOUR TRUST.

What I needed was not a fantasy but *a dream*. You can trust a dream. Dreams link with passions and draw out the best in a person. But they require lots of energy. Every new creation is, first, a dream, or spiritual creation, before it becomes physical. The transformation requires sacrifice and a strong will. As they say, "you gotta wanna," because making dreams into reality takes hard work. And thank God that it does. Imagine if every wacko's dream came true the instant he thought it up! Even God takes no shortcuts but uses the energies inherent in the natural universe to create with.

Of course, nature is like putty in God's hands. Human nature is more stubborn, I've found. At least *mine* is. I had this Venus-like image of myself plastered like a fresco to the inside of my cranium, and I like to have thrown a tantrum at the mere suggestion that I'd have to *work* to make it reality. *Spoiled?* Just call me Cleopatra: Queen of Denial. But this queen was like the emperor who had no clothes on—if you get my drift—and Doc Lowell didn't hesitate in pointing that out.

So. I'd made a fool of myself with a fantasy; let's see what I could make of myself with a dream . . .

DREAM ON

You guessed it—Doc Lowell's diet plan didn't work. I tried—I really *tried*! But after three days of using cups, half-cups, and quarter-cups to measure out my food and losing zero pounds, I gave it up. Then I tried a revolutionary diet from *The National Enquirer* until one day, I knew I'd heave at the sight of another grapefruit. Then I tried a diet of chicken livers and apple peels from *The Mike Douglas Show*. The day after that, I switched to a diet a friend lost twelve pounds on in ten days. I gained three pounds in two days. But I didn't give in. I started a quest for the perfect diet, and over the following months tried every diet I could sink my teeth into. I tried the powdered milk shake diets, the nectarine-and-rice diet. I tried the meat-only diet and the seaweed diet. I took pills. I counted calories. I counted carbs. I counted grams. I tried a liquid diet for forty days and forty nights. I even dabbled in self-hypnosis: "*Ice-cream is frozen pond scum . . . pond scum . . . pond scum . . .*" Nothing worked. I even tried going on several diets simultaneously, hoping they'd have a cumulative effect. They did. In a year, I lost the same thirty pounds three times over! I lost and gained. Lost and gained.

"Look, Joan," Doc Lowell said, when I visited him again, "I have to speak frankly."

"Uh-oh," I said. "I *hate* it when doctors speak frankly."

He ignored me. "Diets don't work by magic, they work by effort," he said. "The diets aren't failing to work, *you* are."

He was right. Just a few days earlier, I had purchased five low-cal dinners from the market's frozen-food bin, planning to eat one each night for the next five nights. But when I got them home, I couldn't decide which flavor to try first, so I ate them all. One after the other, down the hatch they went, because I thought the next one, then the next one, then the next would be the one to satisfy me.

"I'm scared, Doc," I said. "I don't have what it takes to mal-nourish myself."

"Well, we can't perform another bypass, Joan. What are *you* going to do?"

Frustration got the best of me, and I snapped, "You're the doctor! What are *you* going to do?" Classic Joan behavior, right? Shirk the blame, shirk the responsibility for the cure.

But the doc was wise. "I'll tell you what I'm going to do," he said firmly. "I'm going to put you in a straightjacket and hand feed you myself."

"Hand *deprive* me, you mean."

"Well, what's the alternative, Joan?" he asked.

The alternative was to return to my prison of fat and become a 400-pound death-row inmate again, but I refused to give him satisfaction by saying it. "Just tell me what to do," I sighed.

A few minutes later I left with another blasted diet plan in my pocket and Doc Lowell's instructions to start exercising. But instead of feeling more committed, I only felt more afraid. The stakes seemed higher now and my confidence lower.

Why is it that when we resolve to change our habits, we are threatened by fear? Fear of failure, fear of weakness, fear of pain. For example, a person resolves to quit smoking and immediately wrestles with a bundle of fears. He or she thinks: Do I want to quit badly enough? How much will it hurt? Will it make me crazy? How bad is my addiction? When I find out, will I lose my resolve? Am I brave enough? Strong enough? Mature enough? How long before it's over? Will I find out something about myself I don't want to know?

And the underlying fear: Could this *kill* me?

For dieters, it's: Could I die of starvation? It's *not* a shallow fear. It's a downright *primordial* fear! When the body thinks it's starving, the same mechanism kicks in today that kicked in when our first ancestors' crops failed. The brain says to the body, "Hold tight to that fat!" because the body can live for a long time off its fat stores. To lose weight, you gotta fight your own instinct to survive. And in this life-nurturing universe, that's as unnatural as trying to feed a baby from a breast implant. Worse, probably.

People with the disease of obesity have the toughest time losing weight but not because they fear their crops will fail. Obese people fear that they themselves will fail. They fear life. They fear *being*. But they believe as I used to—that if only they can stick with a diet long enough, they'll lose the weight, life will change for them, and they'll be happy forever. They don't realize that food has absolutely nothing to do with being fat. Obesity is an illness of the soul. And because it is, weight loss is not its cure—no matter how hard a person wants it to be.

I'm telling you that you can starve fat off, pill it off, liquid it off, whack it off with a rusty machete, tie a dead cat to a string and hang it around your head under a full moon, or stick

113
▼

voodoo pins into Barbie dolls—but nothing makes a difference, unless you forget about your outsides and deal with your insides. It's an unhealthy soul that creates unhealthy eating habits.

It's the same with any addiction.

HEAL THE SOUL, CURE THE HABIT.

I had to learn this, eventually, or I'm convinced I would not be alive today. Unfortunately, I had to suffer a lot to learn it.

THE SOUL CRIES OUT THROUGH THE BODY, USING ACHES
AND ILLNESSES FOR WORDS.

After my visit with Doc Lowell, I continued my struggle to lose weight, but my body wasn't about to go down easily. One day, it tried to take me down with it.

SEIZURE THE DAY

I started feeling sick. Not just any sick, but sick-like-I-was-going-to-die kind of sick. I visited a friend one day, and I told her, "Debbie, I'm dying." And she asked, "How do you know?" I said, "I know my body, and I know I'm dying."

Then I went to a local doctor, and I said, "I'm dying." And he said, "How do you know you're dying?" And I said, "I just know." Then he told me, "It's your imagination. You're not drinking enough water." And I said, "May*be*, but I'm sick and I'm dying, and it's not my imagination, and I *doubt* that it's the water."

A few mornings later, I got out of bed, and stabs of pain seized my abdomen and dropped me to the floor. I clutched my stomach and let out a cry. Then a wave of excruciating pain hit me and everything went black.

An ambulance took me to the nearest hospital, but the doctors there couldn't determine what was wrong. They put me back into the ambulance and sent me to another hospital. Those doctors were stumped as well. Two of them consulted with each other endlessly and then came into my room and said, "With your permission, Miss Fountain, we'd like to perform exploratory surgery to find . . . "

"Excuse me," I cut in. "Who *are* you two? Lewis and Clark?"

"Uh, of course not, Miss Fountain, but . . ."

"You guys are *not* gonna exploratory nothin' with me." I tried to get up. "Let me out of here!"

"Wait, Miss Fountain." They tried to stop me. "We don't advise . . ."

"That's right," I cut in, again. "You don't. I need my own doctor—Doctor Lowell in Oakland. He'll know what's wrong."

Lewis and Clark got on the phone and informed Doc Lowell of my symptoms, and Doc said, "Send her here, immediately." So the doctors put me on a gurney and the ambulance driver and attendant wheeled me back out.

"Tell me where we're going," the driver said before sliding me into the back of the ambulance.

"Kaiser Hospital, in Oakland," I said.

"I've never been there."

"You've never been to *Kaiser?*"

"No, but you can tell me how to get there."

"Oh, for heaven sakes!" I climbed off the gurney. "Let me ride up front. I'll show you how to get there!"

We arrived in just over an hour. Doc Lowell had guessed what was wrong and was waiting. He sent me immediately for X-rays, which, upon examination, confirmed his suspicions.

"It's serious, Joan," the doc said. "A piece of the bowel we bypassed two years ago is diseased. We've got to get it out."

"I have a diseased bowel?" I asked.

"It happens," he said. "The empty bowel gets kinked, and the kink restricts blood flow. If the bowel dies, there can be dangerous complications."

"Is it dead, yet?" It felt peculiar, asking this about my own bowel.

"It appears so. The results of your blood tests show signs of massive infection. Your file says you're allergic to penicillin."

"Yes."

"And other antibiotics."

"All of them."

The look on Doc's face made me afraid. "We can't waste any time, Joan," he said. "Will you let me operate?"

"It sounds like my only choice."

Within an hour, I was in surgery. This time, no flights through the void, no oneness with the universe—I just woke up sometime later in a private recovery room full of blaring lights and buzzing machines.

The doc was standing near my bed. "How do you feel, Joan?"

"Like I've been operated on by a pack of wild mules."

"Sorry. We tried to be gentle. We cut five feet of bowel out of you, Joan. It was badly deteriorated and should have come out long ago." He sighed heavily. "You need to know that . . . the decomposed tissues have poisoned your system. It's almost impossible to fight off that amount of infection without antibiotics."

"Nothing comes easy in my life."

"Your condition is very serious. We have the best facilities, the best equipment, and the best personnel. You'll have every possible chance to pull through."

"I'm not slim, but my chances *are*. Is that what you're telling me?"

"I'll know more in the morning, Joan."

He told me to rest and left the room.

Meanwhile, my mother and two younger sisters, Rose and Pat, sat out in the waiting room. I should remind you that I'd been away from home for ten years, now. Rose was twenty-five and Pat twenty-two. They had visited my house during the years after my first surgery, and we had partied and had great times together. With our father's death—and I'll write about that soon enough—our relationship had begun to heal. As for Momma, she'd been warming up to me, too, but slowly and in her own silent way. It was my sister Rose who related what happened when Doc Lowell went out to tell them I was dying.

Doc: I'm Joan's surgeon, Doctor Lowell. Thank you for coming so quickly.

Rose: Pat can get some surprising speed outta that old car when she's got a good excuse. Even Momma agreed she should drive this time.

Pat: Any excuse to frustrate the CHP.

Rose: When can we see Joanie?

Doc: Later this evening. I just came from the IC unit, and she's resting. We've listed her in critical condition.

Pat: The nurse told us.

Doc: We're doing everything we can, but when your sister arrived, the infection was already widely spread. Without antibiotics, it's doubtful she'll make it until morning. I'm very sorry.

Pat: Make *what* till morning?

Rose: Yeah, what is it she's not supposed to make?

Doc: Uh, pardon me?

Pat: You said she won't make *it* till morning, and I wondered what *it* is.

Doc: Well, she . . .

Pat: I should tell you that I've got Raiders tickets for this weekend, and I know nothing will happen to make me miss that game.

Rose: Doctor, you tell Joanie that Pat's got football tickets. She knows better than to mess with *that*.

Pat: Besides, I've got nothing I can wear to a funeral.

Rose: Me neither—so there just ain't gonna *be* one. You tell her *that*, too. Whatever it is she's not supposed to make, well, doctor, you just forget about that.

According to Rose, it took Doc Lowell a minute to catch on. As a family, we've had our troubles, but as individuals, we're *strong*. We've got *strong* frames, *strong* blood, *strong* genes, and *strong faith*! We're descended from those who survived crossing the Atlantic in disease-infested slave ships, and Pat and Rose just figured we were all pretty much immune to any lesser threats. Maybe my sisters didn't understand the seriousness of my condition, but they saw no sense in talking about me not making it till morning. They knew I would. And they refused to let Doc Lowell say anything contrary. Momma—sitting straight in her chair—kept quiet, but her daughters spoke well enough for her. Finally, Doc Lowell understood these three women and their combined message of faith:

MORNING ALWAYS COMES.

Doc: Well. I see you *are* Joan's relations. I'll tell the staff you'll be joining her for breakfast.

119
▼

TO LIFE

When morning came, Momma, my sisters, and I did have breakfast together, or rather, they ate scrambled eggs and flapjacks while I watched my IVs drip. Rose told me about Doc Lowell trying to "break the news" the night before. "I'll bet," she said, "he's not used to having patients prove him wrong."

I said, "He never told *me* I wasn't supposed to make it, so it's not my fault." But I knew my condition must have been nip and tuck. All night long, a nurse had sat nearby, monitoring me closely. Doctors checked my condition regularly. I slept fitfully—because of the pain—but I wasn't afraid of dying. My sneak preview had cured me of that fear. If I was to die in the night, I knew I'd go further than near-death this time—I'd go all the way. But that was okay—I could live with dying.

The question was: could I live with living? Since I was eight, my body and I had been at odds. Now it was trying to kill me with lethal infection just to prove a point. But I wanted to beat this poison. To do it, I'd need stronger medicine than what leaked into my bloodstream from the trio of IV bottles near my head.

"Did you guys bring cards?" I asked.

Pat said, "Of course we brought cards, girl! You up for a game?"

"If I can play lying down. But you have to promise not to go easy on me."

"Hah!" Rose laughed. "You could be on your last breath, and Pat wouldn't throw a game your way."

Pat produced a deck. She shuffled and dealt a three-hand game of bidwist while Momma sat in a corner chair and read her Bible. I caught Momma's eye, and she gave me a faint grin. It was then that I knew I'd make it to see another morning, even if it had to come one game of cards at a time. There's nothing so reassuring as a mother's smile and a cardshark sister's taste for your blood.

By the end of the next day, my condition hadn't improved. Doc Lowell remained silent about my odds, preferring "wait-and-see" over showing enthusiasm that I was still alive. My sisters had grown tired of playing Deathwatch Bidwist during the day and sleeping on waiting room couches at night. They decided to take Momma and go home.

"Notify us if she flat-lines," Pat joked with Doctor Lowell, then jabbed a finger at his nose, "but not during Friday's game."

That night—my third in intensive care—was filled with fever and terrible pain. They gave me morphine, which brought haunting visions of watching my body die and decay, one piece at a time. Around midnight, I woke up in a sweat, startled by the pressure of someone's hand on my shoulder.

"Hello, Joan. It's all right." It was the nurse with the white hair ribbon. "I need to take your temperature."

"You're still here," I said weakly.

"Actually, my shift just started." The sound of her voice made my nightmares fade.

"I remember you from two years ago," I said.

121
▼

"I'm sorry, I often remember faces, but . . ."

"It's okay, I had a different face back then. I've lost a lot of weight." By now, I felt the cold sweat receding.

"That's wonderful." She stuck a thermometer in my mouth and updated my chart with numbers glowing from an instrument panel near my head. Then she removed the thermometer and added the results to my chart. "Are you comfortable?" she asked.

"No," I said. "I'm restless. I've been lying in this bed for days, and it's starting to feel like a coffin."

"Can I get you another pillow or something?"

"What I really need is to stand up for a minute."

"You're too weak. I'm afraid you'd fall."

"You could hold on to me."

"I'm sorry. I can't let you up without Doctor Lowell's okay. Maybe in a day or two."

I wouldn't give up. If I could communicate my feelings to anyone, it would be to this woman, whom I knew to be as compassionate as any person I'd ever met. "Doctor Lowell considers it a miracle that I'm still alive," I said. "I believe I can fight this infection, but if I could get out of this bed and stand up— just for one minute—I'll know I can fight it."

Her eyes softened.

"Please, just for a minute," I said. "I need to feel alive."

She smiled, closed the door, and drew the curtains across my window. She pulled the IV tubes and monitor wires away from the side of my bed, then popped the safety bars down. She pressed a control that lowered the bed to about two feet from the floor, then raised the head until I was practically sitting up straight.

"All right." She spoke softly. "Let's take this slowly. We

don't want to ruin Doctor Lowell's beautiful stitchery."

She folded back the blankets and pulled my knees slowly to the edge of the bed. She wrapped an arm around my shoulders and helped me to my feet.

I drew in a sharp breath.

"Are you okay?" she asked, steadying me.

I winced. "The floor is *cold*."

"That's good," she giggled. "At least your feet are alive."

"Anyone for a midnight stroll?" I grinned.

"I'm good for a few miles," she said. "But you have to carry your own catheter bag."

I let out a laugh that turned into a cough. "Thanks," I said. "No, really. Thanks for this. I feel better already."

"Yes. I can see it in your face," she said and hugged me. A minute later, she tucked me into bed again and put the tubes and the machines back where they were. She drew open the curtains and turned to go, but stopped. "Life looks good on you, Joan," she said and walked out.

I slept soundly the rest of the night.

The next day, Lynette came to visit.

"The nurses weren't going to let me in," she said, "but I told them I was your sister."

"Oh, good," I said. "I always wanted a white sister."

"Poor nurses. All their patients must get to looking the same after a while," she said. "How you doing, Joan? You're still on the critical list."

"Doc Lowell's being stubborn. He just doesn't want to admit I'm going to make it."

"You have to make it because guess what?" Her eyes lit up. "Boz Skaggs is coming!"

123
▼

"When!" I almost leapt out of bed but then thought of the unpleasant effects that dislodging my catheter tube would have.

"He's coming in three weeks," she said.

"Lynette, you *have* to get us tickets."

"Will you be out of here by then?"

"If anything can help me get out of here quicker, honey, you know it's tickets to a Boz Skaggs concert."

"Then we're *going*!" said Lynette.

She turned to the nightstand and filled two paper cups with water. "To The Boz!" she said, handing a cup to me.

"To life," I said, and we drank up.

A PRAYER OF A CHANCE

The next morning, Doc Lowell came in, and from the expression on his face I knew he had bad news.

"Joan," he said, "I hate to tell you bad news."

"Then don't tell me, charade it to me," I said. "I hate bad news, and I'm lousy at charades. It could take me days to figure it out."

"We don't have days. I want you back in surgery first thing tomorrow."

"Again? If you remove any more intestines," I told him, "I won't be able to get a foot away from a toilet for the rest of my life!"

"It's not that kind of surgery, Joan. I want to give you a colostomy."

"Oh. A colostomy." I was relieved, at first. "Well, you must have decided that I'm going to live. You wouldn't be giving a colostomy to a woman who's dying."

"Who says you're dying?"

"The critical list."

"You're off it."

"I am?"

"We're moving you upstairs to a regular room this afternoon."

"And I thought you had *bad* news for me!"

"Joan, do you know what a colostomy is?"

"Yes, you drill a hole in my gut, and instead of using a toilet, I poop out that hole into a little plastic bag."

"For the rest of your life," he added. "A colostomy is permanent."

"At least I've *got* a rest-of-my-life," I said, smiling. "A colostomy is a fair trade, I'd say."

But after Doc left, I got thinking, and my enthusiasm dimmed. Before this news, I had believed I would fully recover, eventually get skinny, and live a normal life. But life with a colostomy was not normal, and all my life, all I ever wanted was to be normal. It wasn't the thought of hassling with tubes and bags for the rest of my life that depressed me; it was knowing that if I had never gotten fat, I would never have needed a colostomy. Now every day for the rest of my life, strapping that little bag to my side would remind me that I was damaged goods and that I had no one to blame for it but myself.

I turned more sour as the morning went on. Later, they moved me to a private room on the fifth floor where, gratefully, the urgent shuffle and the noise of the ICU were missing. But my room felt lonely as the day wore on. All I could think of was the next day's surgery, and my heart sank deeper and deeper under its terrible significance. Realizing I needed to have someone near me, I phoned my mother at work.

"Momma, I'm scared," I said when she answered. "Can you come?"

"What's the matter, Joan?"

"They're doing a colostomy on me tomorrow, and it's terrible. I feel terrible."

"I'll come when I can," she said.

"When you can? Momma, they're going to operate on me! I'd feel better if you would come."

"I can't get off work now, Joan. I'll be there tonight, though. Sometime."

I felt almost hysterical. "Momma!" I cried and then realized she'd already hung up. I put the phone down, grabbed a pillow, and yelled into it. The next several hours were torture. I watched the clock, aching for Momma to get there, but dreading the coming of night. Following the night would be the morning and my third encounter with Doc Lowell's knife. It was all I could do to stay in my bed, but finally, around eight, Momma walked through the door, and I was never happier to see her.

She approached my bed. "Here," she said softly, producing a Thermos from her large purse. "I brought you some chicken broth."

Momma was her usual distanced self—no cheery "Hello, dear" or "I'm sorry, I came as soon as I could." But I felt so relieved to have her there, I wasn't bothered.

She popped off the Thermos cup and filled it with brown, steamy liquid. "Maybe this will calm you," she said and handed it to me.

I took a sip. "What's in this?" It tasted good, but not like chicken broth.

"Restorative herbs and a pinch of chicken."

Oh, *health-food* broth. I might have guessed. "Maybe I should put it in an IV bottle and take it in straight through the veins."

Momma sat in a chair, pulled out her Bible, and began reading silently. I drank the broth and relaxed into my pillows. Then I watched her for a time. Her face, wrinkled now by age, appeared composed and serene as her eyes shifted across the page. I drew upon her serenity, and much of my anxiety melted away. We didn't speak, but oddly, by her silence, Momma comforted me. In the past, I would have accused her of ignoring me. But tonight, I doubted those accusations and wondered if it was I who had been oblivious to her silent offerings all those years. What was it with Momma and her Bible, I wondered. My trauma with Jerome and the little Gideon Bible hadn't happened yet, so I didn't understand my mother's attachment to her Bible. I believed in God, and I felt connected to my Baptist religion, but my mother possessed a spirituality I was never acquainted with myself. It had something to do with that Bible of hers.

The hour grew late, and visiting hours ended. Though we'd hardly exchanged words, Momma's visit seemed complete, somehow. She stood, put away her Bible and Thermos, then placed her hand on mine.

"Will you pray for me, Momma, before you go?" I asked.

She closed her eyes and breathed a simple prayer: "Oh, Lord in heaven, comfort my daughter in her darkest hours. And may we ever rejoice in Thee and in Christ Jesus. Amen."

I thanked her, and she slipped her purse over her arm and left.

A nurse entered and settled me in for the night. She turned the light out, and soon the entire ward grew quiet and dark as, one by one down the hall, lights in the other rooms went out, too. I lay staring toward the ceiling, feeling not so much afraid anymore of the morning as resigned to it. But the longer I lay, the heavier my earlier sadness settled over my heart. I thought: This surgery will be a tragedy that should never have happened. And yet, how could I have avoided it? I felt I'd been heading straight for it all my life—or at least since I was eight.

These thoughts would not let me sleep. Far into the night, I lay awake, aching for a way to change my life's inevitable course and feeling my heart breaking because I knew it was too late for a change.

I wished Momma had not left me, and I looked for a Bible in the drawer next to my bed. She'd always told us to read the 91st psalm when we needed comforting. "Momma, my best friend hates me," one of us would say. "Read the 91st psalm," she'd answer. "Momma, some kid stole my money." "Read the 91st psalm." "Momma, the house is burning down." "Read the 91st psalm." But I could find no Bible in the drawer. So I turned to the other thing Momma always taught; I prayed for God to see me through this blackest of nights. I let my prayer play over and over in my head, and I tried to relax.

129
▼

Had I fallen asleep? I opened my eyes at the sound of a voice in my room. There, in the dark, was a man sitting where Momma had sat only hours before. The man was black, had short cropped hair, and wore the white uniform of a hospital orderly. He held a small book in his lap and was reading from it out loud. I should have been alarmed and fumbled for the button to call a nurse. But the man's voice was soothing and I felt unafraid. There was no light to read by, but his words came steady and sure. Maybe, I thought, he was repeating the phrases from memory. I recognized them as passages from the New Testament. I wondered if he were a volunteer or an orderly on break, but I didn't stop him to ask. The comforting words flowed over me, and soon the man's gentle voice had lulled me into a deep and peaceful sleep.

"Good morning, Joan."

I awoke with a start.

Doc Lowell poked his head through the door. "I've got some med students in the hall. Do you mind if they observe your pre-surgical checkup?"

The clock on the wall read 10:30. The hospital was bright and bustling again. I'd slept a good long time. "Okay with me," I said and tried to shake off my grogginess. I looked at the chair where the orderly had sat reading in the dark. No sign of him.

Doc Lowell lead the group of six interns toward my bed. "This patient's name is Joan Fountain," he said. "She's twenty-seven and suffers from a collapsed bowel, peritonitis, and the effects of severe systemic infection. She's scheduled for a colostomy in a few hours."

The students, in their lab whites, surrounded my bed. They looked bored, as though Doc Lowell were lecturing them on the physiological properties of toenail clippings. A few of them, however, perked up when he donned a latex glove and asked me to roll over.

"Don't mind this crowd, Joan," he said. "We'll keep you covered with the sheet."

A few shoulders sagged, and I dutifully rolled over.

The doc began. A moment later, he spoke to the students. "Um . . . would everyone wait out in the hall for me, please?"

They filed out, and I said, "Is something the matter?"

"Would you turn onto your side, Joan? I just want to check again here."

I did, and he did—this time pressing his other hand into my

lower abdomen. It didn't hurt, except when he pressed near my incision.

"Ow!" I said and swatted his hand.

"Sorry." He held motionless for a minute. "You know what?"

"Your finger's stuck?"

"No." He quit probing and washed up at the corner sink. "I'm going to order some tests and send you to X-ray. I need a clearer picture of what's going on."

"What is it, more bad news?"

"If I return and ask to play charades, you'll know."

He walked out, and my heart started thumping at the slam of the door.

What was wrong with me *now*? Did the doc suspect cancer or something? A nurse came in and drew blood. An orderly carted me to X-ray and back. Through it all, I imagined the worst: that I had only three weeks to live, or that I had *years* but would suffer an ugly, lingering death. I even imagined that I'd developed some kind of radical syndrome and would have to be quarantined inside a glass cage where doctors and scientists from all over the world could gather to observe my death. *That* would be fitting, I thought. Part of me always knew I was a freak in life. Why not in death, too?

131
▼

A nurse came in to change my dressings, and I asked her about the man who read to me during the night.

"A man was in your room? About what time?" she asked, pulling the bandages away from my stitches.

"Sometime after midnight," I said. "He looked about forty, I'd say, kind of smallish—maybe five-six, a hundred and fifty pounds."

"There's a nurses station right outside. Only a doctor or

nurse could get by that late. How long did he stay?"

"I don't know. He was just there, and then I fell asleep. Maybe he's an orderly on the night shift."

"Male orderlies aren't allowed in women's rooms at night. There's a strict policy. Imagine the lawsuits!"

"Well, it was dark. Maybe he thought it was a man's room."

She cleaned my incision with a warm sponge and started applying new wrappings. "You said he was black?"

"With short hair, almost a buzz cut. If you find him, tell him thanks. He really helped me to sleep."

"Your description doesn't fit anybody I've seen, but I'll ask around." She finished up.

The man had such a warm and healing influence on me, I hoped he'd come back. If he did, I'd promise not to give him away. I loved the idea of a guy sneaking around the dark hospital and comforting patients by reading the Bible to them. Just thinking about him made me less afraid of what news Doc Lowell might bring. And it wasn't twenty minutes later that I learned what that news was.

"You awake?" Doc's face appeared through the door. He wasn't smiling.

I nodded, and he walked towards me carrying a thick folder. I assumed it was my medical records.

"How're you feeling?" He came around to the far side of the bed where there was room enough for him to sit down—right on the mattress.

"I'm feeling fine," I said, shifting a little to make room for him. "But I've never had a doctor in bed with me before. So, tell me. How *should* I be feeling?"

He put the folder down and brought a knee up so that he could face me directly. He just stared at me for a minute.

"What *is* it?" I said.

He sighed and shook his head.

"Is this a charade?"

"No." He ran a hand through his hair a few times. "This is a mystery. You're fine, Joan. I mean, you're *fine*."

"Yes, I'm fine," I said. "What's the problem?"

"*That's* it. You're fine. You're cured. Completely. No peritonitis, no collapsed bowel, no infection. You're cured."

"I'm cured?"

"You can go home."

"I can?"

"I've already signed the release."

"I don't understand," I said. "What about the surgery?"

He grinned for the first time and shook his head.

I had to make sure. "No colostomy?"

More grinning and shaking. "I've never seen this kind of spontaneous healing," he said.

"The tests and the X-rays?"

"Tests positive. X-rays clean," he said.

"How?" I was lost.

"I don't know, Joan. I've been in medicine for almost thirty years, and still the human body surprises me."

"You're saying I can really *go home*?"

"I want you back for a checkup in a week, but in the meantime, you're gone, lady!"

He leaned over and hugged me, and I made a quick mental check of my body.

How do I feel?

I feel good.

Do I have pain?

No pain.

How's my gut?

Feels normal for a gut. No kinks. No cramps.

The infection?

No sense of disease or poison anywhere.

I feel whole.

I feel healthy.

I feel a little tired, but alive.

Yes. I feel definitely *alive!*

And then I felt *happy*, and I hugged Doc Lowell hard. "I'm over it," I said. "I'm really healed. What did you do?"

He released me and sat up. "I just cut you into pieces, Joan. Somebody else put you back together. It's a medical mystery."

A mystery? Then I remembered the Phantom Bible Reader, and some of the words he read echoed in my ears:

"Thou shalt not be afraid for the terror by night; nor for the arrow that flieth by day; . . . For he shall give his angels charge over thee. . . . He shall cover thee with his feathers. . . . He shall deliver thee."

These words hadn't come from the New Testament as I had believed—they were from the 91st psalm. I should have known. And I should have known my mother to be in league with angels. This healing was no mystery—it was a *miracle*. The Creator had used Momma's prayer, maybe even her broth, and the gentle words of an angel in the dark to heal me as I slept.

WITH THE CREATOR, THERE ARE NO MYSTERIES—ONLY MIRACLES AND MERCIES, SMALL AND GREAT.

Doc Lowell remained silent for a moment, holding my

hand. I didn't tell him about my visitor in the night, but judging by his thoughtful grin, I believe he sensed more miracle in this mystery than he wanted to admit. "This thing that has happened to you, Joan, is rare and unexplainable," he said. "It's very, very special. You should respect it and honor it by taking better care of yourself. Your body has given you a new chance. Don't take that for granted."

I nodded, unable to speak.

"I'll see you in a week," he said and walked out to attend to his other patients.

I knew they'd all find him smiling.

TIRE TREAD AND DANDELIONS

As much as I believe that NOTHING BAD HAPPENS, EVER, I also believe that NOTHING GOOD HAPPENS, EVER, WITHOUT A PURPOSE. I should have died in that hospital, so coming away with only a colostomy would have been miracle enough. But The Creator had a purpose for saving me from even that. God doesn't send angels for no reason, you know. Twenty years have passed, and that reason is still unfolding itself to me. "Some miracles take time" I've heard it said. So also do the purposes behind some miracles—they ripen as we grow. Until one day— if we've watched carefully—we'll see the fruit of miracles, and we'll taste that fruit, and it will fill us with pure joy.

PATIENCE AND FAITHFUL EXPECTATION REVEAL THE GOOD IN ALL THINGS.

One day I'll see the fruit, taste the joy, and understand completely why I'm still living in this skin. For now, I only know that I belong in it and that I'm loved and that my life is not wholly my own. Because of this, I expect more miracles to pop up now and then. And they do—as they do for everyone. Whether we acknowledge them as such or not, The Creator's tender mercies are all around us. We breathe. Children learn to walk. The downhill course of water remains predictable. Cool weather allows peach trees to set fruit. These illustrate a facet all miracles share:

MIRACLES DON'T SPRING FROM LIFE, LIFE SPRINGS FROM MIRACLES.

This should teach us a thing—or three—about life. First: where miracles are not, life is not. Second: our existence depends in every way on The Creator's free and loving graces. And third: there can never be so many trials in life as to crowd out all the miracles.

We ought to consider these and wise up, my friends.

We ought to quit focusing on impossibilities and open our eyes, instead, to miracles.

We ought to become like the yellow dandelions that rise from cracks in the pavement on busy freeways; though adversity threatens us on every side, we ought to turn our faces upwards to the sun, share our beauty and our gifts with others, and every day *thank God* that we're alive!

137
▼

PART SEVEN

▼

No one can make you feel inferior without your consent.

Eleanor Roosevelt

JOAN FOUNTAIN'S BODY AND SOUL

Days after Doc Lowell discharged me from the hospital, I became super devoted to a new diet and exercise program. One morning I just woke up inside the body of an aerobics freak, and within a year I had grape-vined and pony-stepped my way down to 170 pounds.

A miracle? Yes, but not a surprising one. If you woke up every day knowing that The Creator had use for you, you'd create miracles, too. Believe me, no triple-supplemental, banana-mango smoothie for breakfast fortifies you better than to wake up knowing your life has meaning.

I not only lost weight, I found work, too—at the Welfare Department. All that experience filling out government welfare forms came in handy after all. But that job didn't last long. One day, Larry, my aerobics instructor at the YMCA, got sick, and I volunteered to sub for him. It turned out that the students liked me better. So, the next day, the director fired Larry and offered me the job. The Richard Simmons in me couldn't say no, and I began a five-year stint, teaching three YMCA aerobics class-es a day. Sometimes I taught a fourth.

Sometime during my second year, sweatin' in unison with folks and yellin' "Pump those knees! Clench them cheeks!" started making me wish for more out of life. During breaks, I developed a nutrition and fitness program of my own. Then, on days off, I presented my program to schools, women's groups, and to clubs. To my surprise, demand for my seminars increased. I created a business—Joan Fountain's Body and Soul—and conducted on-site fitness seminars for businesses and employee associations. I went on the radio and became known as a kind of local health guru. Newspapers featured me, and eventually I was given a regular spot on television where I demonstrated low-fat cooking techniques.

Yes, people, that gorgeous black lady on the TV screen was me—the same Joan Fountain who played Hide-and-Don't-Seek at home for two years. Teaching aerobics had firmed up my self-confidence as well as my hindquarters. It helped me discover I had a pinch of charisma—gifted by The Creator—because in front of an audience, I came alive. I connected. Lights, camera, flash that famous Joan Fountain smile, and people all over the city tuned in, even when I said something like: "Hi, all you calorie-conscious cuties at home! Today, our low-fat recipe is whey-solids burgers with eggplant dressing. And believe me, they're *to die* for!"

Well, I believed they were to die for at the time.

"Hello, Momma." I phoned her one night. "Have you seen me on TV yet?"

"Rosie mentioned it." Momma sounded tired.

"I have a cooking spot three times a week during the news."

"I don't watch the news."

"I know, Momma, but I've adapted some of your recipes."

She sighed. "I'm usually at work."

"Remember those health books you had when we were little?"

She didn't answer.

"I guess they stuck with me all these years."

Still no answer.

"Momma?"

"What."

"How are you, Momma?"

"I just pray for strength . . . pray for strength."

"Tell Rosie to call me if you need anything, Momma. I'm not far away, now."

"Oh, I'm fine," she said. "Don't need nothin'—only God's love."

"I know that. I know." I breathed deeply. "Well, I guess I'll go. You'll catch me on TV someday, I'm sure. There's plenty of time. I'll call you maybe next week, Momma."

No response.

"Momma?"

She'd hung up.

Over the next three years, the YMCA and Joan Fountain's Body and Soul occupied every minute of my days. Interesting word: *occupied*. If passions feed us and addictions consume us, I suppose it's our occupations that occupy us. Sad—because who we are is revealed by what occupies us. There would be less mental illness and stress in this world if our professions professed our real selves.

RICH ABUNDANCE FLOWS FROM RICH SELF-EXPRESSION.
SCARCITY FLOWS FROM SELF-OCCUPATION.

But fitness was not only my new occupation, it was my new addiction, too. I had traded getting fat for getting fit. Of course, I didn't know this. I saw that foxy goddess in the mirror, and I thought she was me—body and soul. Remember what I said? Never trust a mirror. That was my body all right, but not my soul. The proof was in the battles I waged with my old foe on weekends. Food.

Fridays, on my way home, I'd stop to buy groceries to last me through Sunday. But you'd think I were shopping for a month by the way I loaded up my cart.

"Having guests this weekend?" a clerk might ask. And I'd answer, "No. I've got a dozen recipes to try out for my cooking class." This lie would never have worked when I weighed 420 pounds. But at 170, it worked like a breeze through the outhouse. Nobody suspected me.

Anyway, by the time I drove those groceries home, the bags would be all ripped up from me trying to get at the food with one hand while steering with the other. Too bad my car didn't have cruise control—I could have steered with my feet and used both hands to grab and gorge. Talk about a road hazard! Somebody should have arrested me for driving under the influence of groceries. But, hey! I'm sorry. With no aerobics classes for two whole days, I *had* to obsess with *something*. And food was safe, now that I worked out enough to keep my hips in check.

When you get soul-cravings, you have to respond in ways that *satisfy*. Otherwise, those cravings come back to haunt you. I hated weekends when the ravenous me returned to roost. I'd eat seven-course meals and kick myself for not having cooked an eighth. The Dunkin' Donuts people could have backed up a truckful of donuts, tipped up the bed, and poured the whole

143
▼

load right down my throat, and I'd ask for seconds. (I tried calling them once for delivery—but they just hung up on me. Too bad, too. I even Got Milk.)

Monday mornings were my salvation—my weekend*ends*. I'd wake up with a whole five days of tortuous aerobics and back-to-back fitness seminars to face, and I'd be delirious. Two seconds into my first class, and I'd forget about my weekend belly-busters. I'd come home and wonder how all those cookies got into my cupboards. (Those Keebler elves are anxiety-prone little imps. I know because they always spent weekends at *my place*.)

Inside my slim and trim new body still lived a little girl in pain. "I'm still here," she nagged. "You'll never be whole. You don't belong. You don't deserve." Her words circled like sharks under the surface of my feelings. If I let anything disturb the surface, they'd strike, and I'd end up a bloody mess. So, even though I knew I had purpose in life, I lived constantly on the edge—careful not to dip my toes too far into reality. I kept myself steady by staying on overload. And I tried to create an image of myself real enough for me to believe in.

Hey! The viewers at home believed in me—body and soul. That made my image real. Right?

Or was appearing fit and strong the worst lie of all?

NO EXCUSES

Aerobics. Aerobics. Aerobics. Aerobics. It gets repetitious. After so many years at the YMCA, I needed to move my act into some other circus tent. When a job offer came from the eating disorders clinic at a local hospital, I said bye-bye to the Y, and I took it. Better pay. More prestige. A hot new image to believe in.

Actually, it was very meaningful work. What I enjoyed about aerobics had not been the shuck 'n jive, but the cheerleading. It satisfied me to push people's limits and then challenge them to go beyond. "Get tough, people!" I'd yell at the peak of workouts. "Your body's gripin' at you right now, but *whatcha gonna do*? Slack or attack? You can *do* this! Take the opportunity to *grow strong*!"

As a counselor at the clinic, I got to cheerlead, too, but without all the sweat.

Life is like an aerobics class. *It* presents the challenges and *we* choose how to handle them. When challenged to endure, do we hang tough or fall back? When challenged with opportunity, do we forge ahead or stay the course? When challenged by the unknown, do we act in faith or react in fear? It all comes down to this:

WE EACH FACE THE SAME CHOICE—TO GROW OR TO
EXCUSE OURSELVES FROM GROWING.

The choice to grow, nobody can steal from us. But we can
give it up. We relinquish it when we blame our nongrowth on
people or circumstances we consider to be beyond our control.
People who struggle with eating disorders or other self-
destructive behaviors do this all the time. They say, "I can't
help acting like this. I have a legitimate excuse." To which I
reply, "If you think you have a legitimate excuse, then you
don't know what an excuse is."

Here's the definition:

AN EXCUSE IS AN ARGUMENT WHICH USES TRUTH TO
JUSTIFY A LIE.

A woman might say, "My mother was mean," which may be
the truth. Then she says, "So I can't expect to have patience
with my own children," which is the lie. Together, they make
up an excuse.

"So many marriages fall apart these days. I could never
commit to marrying someone."

"Work is too stressful. If I didn't smoke, I'd go crazy."

"If I stuck up for myself, my husband would leave and I'd
lose everything."

All illegitimate excuses.

From my first day at the Eating Disorders Clinic I made a
difference because I knew all the excuses. I'd been a disorderly
eater myself most of my life—still was on weekends—and I'd
used every excuse in the book. I knew about lonely. I knew
about anxious. I knew about afraid and about mistreated. I

knew about not fitting in, not measuring up, and not feeling loved. I knew hundreds of ways to justify staying on the hurtful course, refusing personal responsibility, letting fear override desire for change.

One of my first clients said to me, "You seem to understand me and what I'm going through."

"I ought to, honey," I replied. "I used to be fatter than you are."

"Oh come on," she said. "I don't believe you."

"It's no fib," I said. "I used to be so fat, I looked like the planet Jupiter in a dress!"

"Really?" she said. "I don't believe it."

I showed her my photo, and her eyes bulged.

"I believe it," she drawled.

Word spread, and suddenly folks knew there'd be no excuses with that counselor named Fountain. Having once weighed over 400 pounds gave me influence at the clinic that other skinny counselors could only dream of. My clients made better progress. All my suggestions for improving the programs were implemented. The director moved me from teaching standard classes to running advanced seminars.

I even got a raise and with it started putting together a new wardrobe for myself. I still ran Joan Fountain's Body and Soul on the side and needed new clothes for public appearances. In sleek new outfits I would mention the clinic and that I, myself, had once weighed over 400 pounds. The number of clients at the clinic blossomed. Soon, we had so many fat people running around that a person had to grease up with Vaseline just to slip through crowded hallways. The clinic's financial condition solidified, and I got another raise. Soon, the guys in suits—or rather smocks—became so pleased with the changes I created,

147

▼

they restructured the clinic, christened it with a new name—the Obesity Recovery Clinic—and gave me first shot as director.

Having a nose for excuses sure pays off.

On the eve of taking over the new Obesity Recovery Clinic, I moved my stuff into my new office and then sat for a while trying out my new chair and desk. I sat there for a long time, getting the feel of that chair and looking out the window at the sunlight fading on the distant hills. As night approached, I sensed my past and all its troubles drifting away into twilight. I'd found a place at last where the past didn't matter anymore, where people even admired me for it. A place in the *professional* world, far removed from the neighborhood of The Big House. I leaned back, lifted one foot—in a purple Gucci pump—and propped it on the sill. "You've come a long way, baby," I sighed loudly to myself.

The office door banged open, and I jerked my foot down and spun around to see who it was. My heart thundered in my chest.

"Past hours, Miz Fountain." It was only the janitor. "Should I turn out the lights?"

"Go ahead, Lee," I breathed. "Don't worry. I'll lock up."

He nodded and left, and I turned back to the window, shocked by my reaction at sitting there with my Gucci pump up. I had felt *guilty*. But it was *my* office, and I belonged there. Didn't I?

I sat a while longer and stewed. The view out the window grew dark, except for the glow from the main hospital across the quad. The foothills had slipped into blackness and with them so had my heart. Where was my elation? Where was my sense of victory? Sitting there should feel more than just far from The Big House. It should feel like sitting at the top of the highest mountain I would ever have the luck to climb. What was missing? Then I knew. I couldn't be satisfied with my new position until somebody acknowledged that I was worthy of it. I needed someone to say, "You made it, Joan. You deserve this new life. You overcame everything, girl. You *belong* at the top!"

But who? Not my mother. She had quit ignoring me—and that seemed acknowledgment enough. My father? He was dead. Then *who*?

That's when I started believing that maybe nothing, nobody could satisfy my cravings for acknowledgment. Maybe my guilt in that chair came from truly not deserving to sit there.

My stomach churned, and I rifled through the desk in search of food—a candy bar, a package of chips, anything to shove into my mouth. But I came up empty.

Where did these feelings come from? I'd gotten good at analyzing my clients' emotions. How could I be so blind to my own? Just that day, I had led a girl through a maze of confusing emotions to find a truth about herself she'd never known before.

So where was my truth?

My head ached. I had to get out of that office. I grabbed my leather briefcase and my matching Gucci handbag, and I slammed the door behind me. Outside in the lot, my car was the only one left—a sorry-looking green Pinto. How I hated that car. I tore open the door, chucked my things in, and ripped my stockings on the seat frame getting in.

"Stupid, ugly car!" I screamed. "Nobody working for a major metropolitan hospital ought to be driving a stupid *Ford Pinto*!" I jammed the key into the ignition, revved the engine, and preceded a cloud of black smoke all the way home.

149
▼

The next day, I bought myself a new car.

Shortly after that, I bought myself a house.

And not long after that, I let Lee, the janitor, introduce me to a man who would claim to love me and would build a pedestal for me to stand on.

The man's name was Jerome, and you know what happened next. The pedestal was not to stand on, but to be knocked silly from. If not for my little Gideon Bible, that pedestal would have become an executioner's block! All because I'd been feeling lonely, anxious, unloved, afraid, incomplete, unacknowledged.

I know. Excuses, excuses.

At least The Creator saw where my excuses were leading me, and he sent those geeky angels to save my hide. I used to wonder why he didn't just tell me, "Don't marry the guy, Joan. It's a mistake." It might have saved me a lot of anguish. Now, I don't wonder. I knew it was a mistake, myself, before I even said "I do." When we bullheadedly make bad choices, we deserve the consequences. Besides, what better way to reveal our weak excuses than to live their effects? Let me tell you, when I found myself huddled on that kitchen floor, stripped of everything that could possibly save my life but that Bible, I gained a new appreciation of my nothingness. Excuses don't cut it with The Creator, and sometimes he reminds us of that. But he's merciful, too, merciful beyond belief. He orchestrates ways for us to learn our lessons without completely destroying ourselves. The trick is to let hindsight help us stick closer to the truth next time. This requires us to accept that we're imperfect and just plain wrong sometimes. If we can't, then hindsight turns into blindsight, we start shifting the blame, and we create all kinds of bogus excuses for ourselves.

WE EXCUSE OURSELVES FROM GROWING WHEN WE
EXCUSE OURSELVES FROM THE TRUTH.

This life is all about getting many chances to grow. Why
waste them on excuses?

POP QUIZ,
READY OR NOT

Study the following and determine whether true or false:

The process for learning life's little lessons goes like this:

Step One: I have a problem.
Step Two: I know what the problem is.
Step Three: I know the solution to my problem.
Step Four: I put the solution to work.
Step Five: My problem goes away.
Step Six: I've learned something.

Okay, which is it? True or false?

If you answered true, I have news for you—*you* need to get a *reality check*, 'cause things just ain't that way!

This is more the way:

Step One: I have a problem. And then again I might not. What if I only *think* I have a problem? What if, instead, I have a solution in disguise? Hmm . . .

Step Two: I know what the problem is. At least I *think* I know—there are lots of ways to see the facts. By the way, what are the facts? *Ohhh . . .*

Step Three: I know the solution. (Don't I?) I'm not sure of the problem, but I *am* sure of the solution. On the other hand, what if I don't need a solution? What if what I *really* need is a *problem? Aaaacccch!*

Forget steps four through six—they're nothing but questions, too. I'm convinced that even the answer to The Mystery of Life is in the form of *a question* and that if we knew what the question was, we'd spend the rest of our lives asking for somebody to please repeat it!

This is what I believe:

LIFE IS ONE LONG POP QUIZ FOR WHICH WE MUST FIGURE OUT NOT ONLY THE ANSWERS BUT THE QUESTIONS AS WELL.

I declare, right here on this page, that I know one of life's biggest questions. It's one that bears repeating because we should never forget what answer we're struggling so hard to find. The question is this: Who am I?

Ask yourself that question. And don't answer with the obvious. You're more than random biochemical ingredients with a name and a face, a set of roles, and a bunch of likes and dislikes. There is more substance to you than meets the eye. It may take a lifetime to discover the complete you because you come to yourself by bits and pieces—and I don't mean because Freddy Krueger has had his way with you. It's because life is full of changes, and it takes a lot of change and a lot of time to discern what is constant in you. You may pin yourself down for a moment, see yourself clearly, but the moment changes, and you slip away from yourself. You surface, slip away, resurface. It's like playing hide-and-go-seek with yourself. But you can't stay forever with your eyes covered, counting. To win, you have to go looking.

In *The Wizard of Oz*, the Tin Man, Scarecrow, and Lion went looking for a heart, a brain, and courage. The object of Dorothy's quest—to return home—seemed the hardest of all to find, until she discovered that the answer lay within her and that it had been there all along. She simply needed to know herself to find it.

As I mature, the need to know myself grows stronger. Many answers about myself I don't have yet. For example, why I keep buying stuff to hang on the walls of my house. Every wall is already crammed with stuff. But that stuff says loads about me. If you walk in and just sit quiet for a while, you'll get to know me. And the first thing you'll know is, "My heck, this lady needs a house with *more walls*." And I agree!

So far, what I *do* know about myself, I like and I trust because every time I'm true to it, I feel serene and joyful. It's when I've forced choices not in harmony with my inner voice of truth that I've caused worse troubles for myself than I started with. If you don't believe that, you will by the time you finish reading my story. Incest is one of the worst tragedies that can happen to a child. But more tragic is never to overcome the effects of it as an adult. The first step to recovery is to ask yourself, "Who am I?" and then be willing to embrace whatever answer pops out of hiding.

Life surely *is* a pop quiz. Whether we're ready or not, we're always in the thick of it. Too bad cheating won't do us any good. In the first place, nobody's got duplicate tests. The right answer for somebody else may be the wrong answer for you. In the second place, the Test Administrator is always watching over everybody's shoulders—which is actually a blessing because if you've got ears to hear and eyes to see, he drops hints.

And there's no waiting around for our tests to be corrected, either. Most times, we get immediate results as we go. "Ooops, goofed on that one." Or, "Yes! I got it!" The hardest questions are, Who Am I? Why Am I Here? Where Am I Going? and How Do I Get There? The answers become clear when we listen to the voice of truth and when we pay attention to our choices and their consequences.

Here are some strategies for passing the quiz:

155
▼

DON'T GET AHEAD OF YOURSELF.
PAY ATTENTION TO WHAT YOU'RE DOING.
FOLLOW THE ADMINISTRATOR'S INSTRUCTIONS.
KEEP YOUR PENCIL SHARP.
ALWAYS DO THE BEST YOU CAN.

PART EIGHT

▼

THE FIRST DAY OF THE
REST OF MY LIFE

I stormed into my therapist's office. "Mary," I fumed, "I want to *kill* somebody!"

I dropped into a chair, and Mary leapt to her desk and fumbled for the proper report forms. When a client expresses the intent to kill, therapists have to report it in triplicate: blue for county, pink for state, and the goldenrod copy for God.

She found the forms, lifted her pen, and asked, "Joan, who do you want to kill?"

I clenched my fists beneath my nose and didn't answer.

She repeated, "*Who, Joan?*"

But rage, like a tornado, had leveled my brain. I couldn't think. I could only feel. I just sat there, seething, waiting for my brain to work again.

Six months had passed since my dangerous encounter—I've never considered it a marriage—with Jerome. Every day since, I'd offered burnt sacrifices to that blessed institution: quick divorce. It felt fine to be living alone again on "P" Street in my little bungalow with the wide porch. Being a spinster, I had decided, was a relief. Besides, I had plenty of friends, plenty of respect at the Clinic. I had a lot to be thankful for.

So why had I started pigging out at nights and not just on weekends? To watch me pack my cheeks, you'd think I were a client at the Obesity Recovery Clinic, not its director. I disgusted myself. In a matter of weeks I had gained thirty pounds. The scales proved what I so wanted to deny: I had gotten out of control again, fixating on food because I feared dealing with my feelings

My supervisors at the Clinic became concerned. They counseled me, asked me to get into therapy. That's when I met Mary. But I continued to gain weight. Finally, a hospital administrator called me in, referred to some clause in my contract based on the idea that only thin people can help fat people lose weight—proper role models and all that—and said that if my weight reached a certain point, I'd lose my job.

Then I got sick again—as sick as when Doc Lowell operated on me to save my life. I couldn't figure what had happened. My health, my job, and everything new I had become was suddenly at risk. How had I gotten back to this old familiar place?

And now this anger, building up for days, consuming me, making me feel that either I, or someone, needed to die.

Mary stood near me. "Joan?" she put a hand on my shoulder. "I've never seen you this angry. Tell me who you want to kill."

I still couldn't answer.

"Just say it," she urged.

From somewhere deep in my gut, the answer came. In a voice I hardly recognized as my own I said, "My father. But he's already dead." I covered my face with my hands and sobbed.

Mary dropped her pen to the desk and sank into a chair

next to mine. She waited until I could speak again. She waited a long time. These were my first tears since I was eight years old. I had an ocean of them to shed.

Getting the words out—that I wanted to kill my father—caused a gate to spring open in my mind. Memories I didn't know I had emerged. Tears rolled down my face, through my hands, down my arms, and twenty-seven years of my life rolled backwards in time.

I am a little girl again, snug in my bed at night. The Big House encloses me in the familiar embrace of its walls. The weight of blankets presses my cheek, and my breath warms the flesh on my face. My eyes open at the sound of my father's voice. He calls my name from the living room upstairs. Then silence. Why does my father call me? He had frightened me with his talk, saying I was the prettiest of all his children. I don't like his voice. He calls me again, and this time I stand up and walk out of my room. It's dark, and I realize how late it must be, but I know my way up the stairs. I peer through the dim light of the living room and spot my father sitting alone on the couch. He holds out a hand, and I go to him. Then he does things which I can't see clearly, but soon my mother has me, and we are heading quickly out of the house. Momma grips my arm and pulls me toward the car. We get in and drive fast through the streets to a hospital. We pull in and stop. Momma takes me out, and we walk through the door where "emergency" glows red, and I want to ask her, what emergency? But Momma has said nothing, and I'm afraid to ask her. A nurse takes us to a room and tells me to get undressed. I find blood in my underpants when I take them off. Momma doesn't explain. She wads them tight and stuffs them inside her purse. When the doctor arrives, she still says nothing, just watches him lift me onto the table, spread my knees, and strap down my feet. The doctor comes

near me, and I feel pain—sharp, intense pain that is too, too much.
But my mother doesn't comfort me. I have to take myself away to a
dreaming-place until he stops. Later, when Momma takes me home,
my father is missing, and I know I never really was the prettiest of all.

There, with Mary beside me, I lived those scenes as if for the first time. They seemed not at all like a dream. They seemed real. I hadn't known memories could be so clear—but they made many other things clear. I understood why I'd become a stranger at The Big House. My father despised me, and my mother turned away, because I became their living reminder of what happened that night. I understood why I had barricaded myself behind a fortress of flesh. Why I had felt undeserving of success. Why I had begged God, at times, to let me die.

161
▼

Finally, I was ready to speak, and for two hours, in a jumble of words that poured out as uncontrollably as my tears, I told Mary everything. She held my hand and cried with me as I spoke. I told her of the lifelong shame I'd carried—how, like a leech, it had sucked me dry of self-worth. I'd always blamed myself for that shame, though I didn't know what I'd done to deserve it. I figured it was simply because I lived, breathed, took up space in a world where I didn't belong.

But no longer. Now I knew the origin of that shame, and my heart filled with rage. "Arthur Lee Fountain!" I cried. "It was you. *You* did this to me!"

I could hardly bear sitting still. I wanted to get at my father, accuse him, beat him, scream my anger at him. But he was dead and out of reach. Then, if he has to be dead, I thought, let the earth heave up his remains and let God breathe fire on his rotten bones. I wanted vengeance. Violence for violence. A dark grave was not enough for my father. I wanted his soul—wherever it was—to suffer my shame. Shame so heavy I abhorred myself and abhorred my body. Shame that made me camouflage myself with fat until I made myself unidentifiable, until my own organs could not support my weight, until blood flowed again from that place he made me bleed.

My father died in a matter of months after the effects of asbestosis made him quit his job. I had been dying from the effects of shame for twenty-seven years. I needed him to know that.

The phone rang, and Mary picked it up. She said a few quiet words and then hung up.

"I'm sorry," I said to her. "I've stayed too long."

"Don't worry about it," she said. "Joan, there's a lot we still need to talk about. This anger is going to camp out for a while before it leaves."

"I don't want it to leave," I said.

"I've cleared tomorrow morning, Joan. Can we talk more about it then?"

I nodded.

"You need someone to stay with you tonight," she said.

"I have no one," I said. "I'll be fine."

"Come home with me then, if you like."

"Thank you," I shook my head. "I have to live with this alone for the rest of my life. I might as well get started."

She walked me to my car, and I drove home. For the first time in a long time, I didn't go right to the kitchen when I walked in the house. I didn't feel much like eating.

WHAT ANGER DOES

I've learned that we remember when we're ready to remember. I asked Mary once why no bells went off when I got old enough to know what incest was; no voices in my head saying, "Hey, Joan, it happened to *you*"; no nightmares of a blurred face hovering over me in the night; no sudden urges to slash razors across pictures of dads. Mary explained that in our subconscious is a mechanism that hides memories too terrifying to cope with. This mechanism protects us until we *can* cope, and then our memories return.

I was thirty-five when my memories returned. I guess I'd progressed—as they say in manufacturing—from "assembly" to "operational status." With a house, a job, a bit of money in the bank, I must have been ready to turn inward and to cope with what was hidden there. At the Clinic, people had shared stories of their own abuse with me, and I had thought, how terrible it must be to be sexually abused! I had gone home night after night and crammed food in my mouth with spatulas, feeling sorry for those victims of abuse, never imagining I was numbered among them.

Remembering brought the incest forward in time, as though it had just happened. I went through all the phases of fresh tragedy: shock, anger, disbelief. Could my memories have been false? I reviewed my mental images with all the special effects of a high-fidelity VCR, searching for inconsistencies or misinterpretations. Backward search, freeze-frame, slow motion, auto repeat, color enhance. But yes, I was really there; the man with me was Arthur Lee Fountain; what happened between us was incest.

Horrified, I wanted to forget again, become naive again. But the images were with me for good. They were jammed into my head. They couldn't be ejected, erased, or denied. I started wishing I had died that night. Wouldn't death have been better than a life damaged by shame and self-abuse? Yet it felt good to think about being damaged. It gave strength to my anger. And the stronger my anger, the stronger my power to survive.

Unfortunately, anger does unsightly things to a person. People noticed.

"You know . . . ," a colleague at the Clinic told me one day, "the clients are calling you Idi Amin in drag."

"So?" I said.

"So, I thought you should know. You *have* been short-tempered lately."

"I don't care," I returned. "This is the new me. Everyone will have to get used to it." As a born-again victim of incest, I felt entitled to my anger. If I couldn't be angry and still win friends and influence people, then I'd be angry and lose friends and offend people. I wasn't about to give up being angry. But I did *give out*. Anger zaps a person's energy more quickly than a four-minute mile in 110-degree heat. It fries your nerves, strains your heart and your muscles, and it injects enough adrenaline into your system to fuel The Rolling Stones on an extended world tour. Anger is exhausting, it corrodes the body.

But even worse:

ANGER DARKENS THE SOUL.

I not only felt worn out physically, I felt weakened spiritually. Our souls can't be hurt by physical forces, including incest and other abuse. Love, truth, and intelligence set our spirits free, but resentment, bitterness, and hate bind spirits and diminish them. Anger is never a good defense—as I had believed—because anger injures the very part of us we seek to protect.

WE HANG ON TO ANGER BECAUSE IT DISTRACTS US SO WELL FROM OUR PAIN.

165
▼

When I ran out of energy, pain stepped up and overwhelmed me. And with it, a sorrow of the deepest kind. Thick depression settled over me like a long dark winter. I entered a season I can best describe by saying my spirit went into mourning.

WHAT LOVE DOES

You're grieving," the therapist said. "That's normal."

"Yeah, but when will it stop?"

"This is not simple grief, Joan—as if somebody had died.
This grief is more complex."

"I wouldn't know," I said. "I didn't have even simple grief
when my father died."

"So, you're grieving for him now . . ."

I wanted to laugh. "No, I'm not grieving for him," I said.
"I'm grieving for me."

"For having been abused by him, I know," she said. "But,
there's more to it."

Yes, I thought, there's more to it. But I didn't want to admit
it to her.

"Come on," Mary said. "What else? Why are you grieving?"

I clenched my lips and shrugged.

"Denial doesn't work in this room, remember?" she said.

Over the months, Mary and I had listed all the ways in
which denial had made me suffer. I had finally seen the hidden
truth about my life, and if I wanted to use it to heal myself, I
had to leave denial behind. It meant ending my vacation from
the truth. Completely. I had to come home. Unpack. Throw

out all my traveling gear. Never run away from the truth again.

Okay. No more denial.

I stared at an empty space on the wall, and my stomach began trembling. "I'm grieving," I said, "because my father should have loved me better."

I put my hands to my face, and I wept long and hard. After all the years, and all the hurt, I still wanted to love and be loved by Arthur Lee Fountain. He was my daddy, and little girls love their daddies and need to be cherished and protected by them. For twenty-seven years I'd craved being worthy of those things—things only a father can give.

"For whatever reason," Mary said softly, "he chose not to love you better. But that was *his* downfall, *his* choice. Not yours. You were an innocent girl."

167

▼

"I was his *daughter*," I cried. "He betrayed that."

"Yes, he did. Incest is a father's worst betrayal. It betrays the child, and it betrays fatherhood itself."

"He resigned as my father that night," I said.

"But do you want to resign as his daughter?" Mary asked.

My eyes teared up again. "I wish I didn't have to, but it's his own fault. Not that I would want a relationship with him, even if he were alive, but I wish I didn't have to turn my heart against him."

"You don't. Not if you accept your wish for what it is. Love is always a choice. But if you choose it, you have to do what love does."

"What?"

"Forgive him," Mary said.

Forgive him? Khh! Years of pain separated my father and me like a vast chasm. To forgive him, I'd have to leap across it somehow and embrace him as if all that pain didn't matter anymore. How could I do *that*? Pain is *supposed* to matter. Besides, my father did the trespassing; shouldn't *he* be the one to cross over to me? If I did the crossing, I'd become twice his victim—and society says never to let someone get the better of you. Someone does you wrong—you litigate. It's the American way. The Bible says "turn the other cheek," but only the weak turn the other cheek. The strong turn the doorknob to their lawyer's office. Right?

And what about the abuse itself? It couldn't be undone by forgiveness. But I would have to give up resenting it. But if I did that, wouldn't I become a traitor to every child who was ever abused? No. I could never stop resenting my abuse. That was too long a leap for this lady to make—even with my trimmer waistline and a running start. I'd sooner take the plunge over the edge of that chasm than welcome incest into my life.

So, maybe I could never get across, never forgive my father. Maybe I'd have to settle for a long-distance truce with him instead. Anyway, why should I forgive him when he never said he was sorry? Maybe in the afterlife he *still* wasn't sorry—how would I know?

Yet, deep down, none of these arguments gave me peace. I suspected that Mary was right. Peace would only come when I could feel free to love my father. If what love does is forgive, then I decided I'd have to give it a try.

And on that very day—the day I decided to try forgiving—I started down the path to my healing. Of course, I stumbled off it many many times. It's a path we have to fumble around a bit in order to find our footing—most of us are out of shape when it comes to forgiveness.

But I'm here to tell you, the rewards are worth the effort. One day, my feet would be firm on that path, my grief and pain would end, and serenity would fill my soul. I would learn the joy of what my Momma and good old Churchill taught: Never, never, never, never give up . . . your willingness to love. It doesn't come cheaply—especially considering the sacrifices required. But Mary's words were right on. Let me say them another way:

NEVER, NEVER, NEVER, NEVER GIVE UP YOUR WILLING-
NESS TO FORGIVE.

ADDED UPON

The harder you pry at a starfish, the tighter it clings to its rock. So it is with people and resentment. The harder I tried to free myself from resenting my father, the tighter I wanted to hold on. I felt vulnerable letting go of bitterness. Like the starfish, I turned my knobby side out and held on for dear life.

There's a whole world of clinging starfish out there—victims of abuse who want to stay victims. They drag their rocks of resentment with them to group whining sessions. They throw consciousness-raising rallies. They fight for recognition as the unfortunate victims of a sick society. I admit, I got caught up in their scene. It felt good to find others like me. I wore an invisible name tag around like a badge of honor. It read, "Hello—My Name Is Joan Victim Fountain." I wore it because I thought my daddy had branded me that way. That because he had victimized me, I could never be anything different.

Today, I deplore the word *victimized*! I'll never identify myself with that label again. "I'm a victim" has become the mega-excuse for all kinds of selfish and irrational behavior. And you *know* how I feel about excuses; they're the dimmer switch on the light of truth. Those who blame their failure in life on being a victim have turned that switch *way down*.

They're in a black hole. What put them there is believing a terrible lie: that abuse diminishes a person.

However, here is the glow-in-the-dark truth:

ABUSE DIMINISHES NO ONE BUT THE ABUSER.

Once abuse ends, so does victimization. The only way it continues is for a person to choose to perpetuate it by keeping alive resentment and fear. Those who view themselves as victims of child abuse view themselves in the past. They need to come current, or they'll never grow up because:

TO ACCEPT ANOTHER'S DISRESPECT OF YOU IS TO DISRESPECT YOURSELF. IT PUTS YOU AT ODDS WITH THIS LIFE-CHERISHING UNIVERSE.

But enough jabbering about being a victim. I can't come down too hard on people stuck in the same hole I once stuck myself into. Most of those people don't even know they're in a hole. You and I should shine the light and show them the way out. More importantly, we should put our efforts where they're needed most: to rescue the true victims—those who suffer daily from ongoing abuse. We can save them, if we're committed and courageous enough. But then they're on their own, once they're safe, to find lasting peace for their souls.

Every person on this planet goes through tough times, loss, adversity, tragedy. We can, every one of us, call ourselves victims of something or other, if we care to. But I don't. Life—every millisecond of it—arises from the grand miracle of creation. We devalue our very natures as children of our Creator when we consider ourselves victims of His Miracle. Besides, if

NOTHING BAD HAPPENS, EVER, then what is there for us to survive?

WE ARE NOT VICTIMS, AND WE DON'T MERELY SURVIVE. WE ENDURE. AND BY ENDURING, WE ARE NEVER DIMINISHED BUT ADDED UPON.

The call to endure hardship is a grace. It grants us opportunity to grow, to add substance to our souls. To resent it is petty and blind.

So what magic makes us let go of resentment? What magic opens our hearts to forgiveness? If you don't know by now, you haven't read this book carefully.

It's *love*, baby! The magic of love. Love transforms all, especially our pain. I'd still resent my father today if I hadn't let love for him squeeze into my heart. When I quit whining about myself and just thought for a minute about him—the *person* him, not the *role* he played in my life—something startling happened.

It began by remembering his death.

MY FATHER INTO THE LIGHT

My father died the summer I graduated from Solano Community College. My mother cared for him at The Big House during his final days. He was only forty-six.

I happened to be at The Big House when he died. A friend from college had given me a ride on her way to visit relatives. But when she dropped me off, I just stood on the sidewalk wondering why I'd wanted to come. I'd only been back a couple of times since leaving for college—a few hours one Christmas, half a day the previous summer. Both times I'd felt like an intruder. I hadn't even been asked to stay for dinner. I remember thinking I ought to just walk away—I had friends in town I could stay with—but something drew me up the walk and onto the shaded porch.

It must have been the heat.

Anyway, one of my brothers got to the door before I did. "Oh, it's you," he said, and he looked me over once—probably to make sure I was as fat as he remembered. My 300 pounds didn't disappoint him. "Why're you here?" he asked.

"No reason," I said. "It's sweltering. You gonna let me in or what?"

"I ain't stoppin' you." He stepped out onto the porch and let the screen door slam behind him. "I'm splitin'," he said and soared over the steps. He hit the lawn running and lit off down the street.

I jerked open the door and went in. Momma was just coming out of the kitchen. She stopped and looked at me. A few hairs were stuck with sweat to the edges of her face. She held a green cup in one hand and a wet cloth in the other. Neither of us said a word. Half-a-breath later, Momma went down the hall toward the back of the house. A man coughed from that direction—a raspy, drawn out cough. My father. I knew he'd been sick. Rose had called to tell me. She'd said he'd probably die in a few months. From that single cough, it sounded like a few weeks would be more accurate. I could tell that Momma had moved Daddy to the back bedroom—the one nearest the bathroom. The rest of the house was quiet.

Great, I thought. I'm alone in the house with a father who's dying and a mother who refuses to talk to me. I plopped onto the couch and decided that if somebody else didn't come home in twenty minutes, I'd leave.

A few minutes passed. Then Momma's voice came from the hall.

"Lean on the wall, Arthur Lee. I can't hold you up."

The shuffling of feet on linoleum told me Momma was helping my father into the bathroom. Daddy was a large man, and I could hear Momma struggling. But I didn't offer to help. Something about helping my father into the bathroom didn't appeal to me. The shuffling stopped, and by the sounds of it, I knew Momma wasn't going to shut the bathroom door. It was too much. I got up to wait on the porch.

"Joanie!" My mother's voice sounded urgent. "Joanie, come in here!" Then, "Arthur Lee. Arthur Lee!"

I walked to the bathroom doorway and looked in. My father was sitting on the edge of the toilet, and his whole frame had gone limp. He was tipping forward off the seat. Momma had him by one arm, trying to keep him from falling.

"Joanie, help me!" Momma looked up, her eyes wide. "Something's wrong with your daddy."

I went in and grabbed my father's free arm. Between Momma and I, we got him upright and then laid him back against the toilet tank. His head flopped over on his chest, and he took a sharp, ragged breath.

"Arthur Lee," Momma practically shouted into his ear.

I waited for his next breath.

"Arthur Lee."

A tremor shook Daddy's body. I felt his arm tremble in my hands. Then the shaking subsided, and every muscle in my father's body went slack. A shot of adrenaline hit my gut, and I knew he had died.

I looked at Momma.

"Help me lay him on the floor," she said, "then go call the hospital."

"He's dead, Momma," I said. "The hospital can't do him no good."

"Just help me," she said and began easing him forward.

"Do we want him face down or on his back?" I asked, annoyed at having to help.

"On his back."

"Then we've got to turn him before we let him down," I said. "Once he starts to fall, we'll have no control." The bathroom

175
▼

was tiny and narrow, and my father was awfully heavy. We'd never be able to roll him over.

We held onto him as best we could, but Daddy didn't go down gracefully. On his way to the floor, somehow the door got kicked shut, and my father's feet ended up against it. His head, at the other end of the cramped room, landed against the bathtub. Momma and I had a dickens of a time getting his legs out of the way so I could squeeze my own fat body out the door.

I felt a little shocked—as anyone does after watching a person die—but I didn't feel one bit sad. I felt nothing, to be honest. I got on the phone as Momma had asked and dutifully called the emergency room.

"You need to come get my father," I said when the guy answered.

"What's wrong with him," the guy asked.

"He's dead," I said.

"You sure? Did his heart stop?"

"He's not breathin'."

"Are his lips blue?"

"Look," I said, "he's a black man. I can't tell if his lips are blue. You come over here and check them out yourself."

"All right, miss. Give me your location."

I gave it, hung up, and returned to the bathroom. Somehow Momma had gotten Daddy's pajamas arranged. She couldn't let the ambulance workers see him indecent; my mother always created a bit of dignity wherever she could. Momma wasn't crying. She just knelt next to Daddy's head and rested a hand on his chest.

I went to the front porch and waited.

When the ambulance arrived, I held the screen door for the two attendants and their gurney. "Good luck gettin' him on

▼

that thing," I said. Those guys looked pretty scrawny to me.

Sure enough. They couldn't even get my father out of the bathroom. I stood back while they tried to lift him. It was futile. They each grabbed a leg and tried to drag him. They huffed and puffed and jerked and yanked, but Daddy just wasn't comin' out of there. I told you he was big man. They couldn't even get towels under him to slide him out. If they could have, there would still be no room out in the hallway for both my father and the gurney. They'd have to drag him down to the living room over the hallway carpet.

The attendants hadn't moved Daddy an inch, and I couldn't stand anymore of their clumsy attempts, I got out of there. A crowd had gathered in front of the house, so I went across the street and watched. The sun was bright, and I raised a hand to shield my eyes.

After a while the attendants brought out their empty gurney and just stood there helpless on the lawn. Finally, five or six neighborhood men went in to get my father. In a few minutes they brought him through the door of The Big House and onto the shaded porch. They stopped for a minute—the sun was so bright I couldn't see what they were doing. Maybe the men had to readjust their grip, or maybe they just needed a breather. Everyone on the lawn, including the attendants, stood silent, watching. Then there was movement on the porch, and the men appeared, carrying my daddy's body—suspended by the arms and legs—down the steps and into the light.

Seeing my father dangling there exposed to the sun sickened me. I wasn't sorry, didn't pity him or feel ashamed. It was more like disgust that I felt—and I didn't like that feeling. The men heaved my father onto the gurney, and I turned away. I walked as fast as I could down the street. I looked back once as the scrawny attendants slammed the ambulance doors shut. A moment later they drove away—without sirens.

I headed up a side alley and walked several blocks to a phone.

"Come get me," I told my friend.

Then I sat down on the hot sidewalk, and I tried to feel nothing again.

RETROFITTING
MY HEART

The word *forgive* can sound outrageous because of the "give." When somebody does you wrong, you want to *take*—take back your stolen innocence or position or possession. Why should you want to *give* anything?

When my daddy died, I had nothing to give him. No love. No respect. No grief. I had no memories of his abuse; still, all I wanted was to push him away from me. I didn't even attend his funeral.

"I won't sit through any preacher's sermon," I told my roommate, Lynette. "What could a preacher say about my father that *I* would want to listen to?"

"Words of consolation," Lynette suggested.

I screwed up my nose. "*Consolation* is for losers," I said. "My father's finally gone from The Big House, and not even Momma can let him back in. I'd say we're *winners* here, not losers. What preacher would say *that*!"

Many years later my therapist, Mary, asked why I didn't go to my father's funeral, and I said, "Because no preacher could have said the things *I* would want said about my father."

"What would you want said?" Mary asked.

"Things I couldn't say in church," I answered. "I would at least have given a warning to people to stay clear of men like him."

"Your mother loved your father."

"Yes," I said. "But in the sixteen years since he died, I've never heard my mother say a word about him."

"Would *she* have warned people about your dad if she had been the preacher?"

"No," I said. "But Momma would have made a great preacher. Why she loved my daddy mystifies me."

Mary suggested that if I wanted to forgive Arthur Lee Fountain, it might help to try to see him through my momma's eyes.

I told her I would try.

It was growing dark by the time I got home that evening. I didn't go inside the house but sat on the porch and watched through the glow of the streetlamps for the stars to come out. I thought about Mary's suggestion, and I thought about my mother—who was probably asleep already in the two-bedroom house she'd bought across town. She had moved out of The Big House after my daddy died.

What made you love him, Momma? I asked silently toward the stars. You stayed with Daddy. Cared for him to the last. You even protected him. Too well, sometimes. You knew what he did to me, yet said nothing to the doctor that night. Nothing to the nurse or the police. Momma, why didn't you? I was your daughter. How could you respond to *incest* with only silence? Silence then and silence now. What could you say to help me understand? What feelings for Arthur Lee made you turn away from your own child?

Then a thought, bold and sure, as if spoken by a voice both from the stars and from within my soul said to me, "Arthur Lee was once a child, too."

And that did it. All my defenses came down. I leaned my head against the steel rim of the porch chair, closed my eyes, and opened my mind to my daddy. Not the grownup Arthur Lee, but the child he once was.

I envisioned him about eight years old, large, even then, for a boy his age. He stood erect on the porch—not my porch or The Big House porch, but the rough birchwood porch of his boyhood home in Jefferson County, Texas. He'd kicked off his shoes—if he had owned a pair—and he wore no shirt, so that the frayed straps of his farmer's overalls pressed into his sturdy bare shoulders. I imagined him jumping up, giving an easy slap to a beam overhead, and landing square-footed, grinning that rakish grin I'd seen a thousand times—the one which caused him so much trouble in his life after he found out its effect on the ladies.

I gazed on that face and tried to find the source of that grin. But I found something else, instead. Something that I'd been too thick-headed to notice when Daddy was alive. I found a hurt little boy looking out through those eyes. A depth behind the sparkle. A pool of darkness I'd seen every day—whenever I looked into a mirror.

My daddy's eyes were *my* eyes. The hurt in them was *my own*.

Everybody always said I had his eyes. Now I saw it, too, and I understood. My father had been abused as a child, as I had been. We had both been betrayed by someone who should have loved us better but could not.

Tears flowed from my eyes, and I hugged myself in pain. But it was shared pain this time. Not just my own.

181
▼

I wondered how much of himself my daddy had seen in me when I was a little girl: His own ease among strangers. His comfort in a crowd, his ready mind, and capable strong spirit. His sharp wit. He said I was the prettiest of all his children. Had he seen the eyes of others drawn to me as they had been drawn to him?

In me, did my father see the lost promise of his own youth? Was incest his drunken and tragic attempt at retribution for what was taken from him in that Texas house so long before?

I reviewed my memories of Daddy. His anger. His bitterness. His depression. His self-fulfilling fear of failure. The alcohol and drugs which dulled his shame. The bar at the south end of Georgia Street. *All* his hurtful and self-destructive ways. And I saw my own ways reflected in his. Jurassic Joan My obsessions with food, liquor, drugs. My fear of living. The abuse of my body. My ruinous attempts to find happiness. The bitter and resentful victim. I realized my father must have suffered at least as much as I. He had inflicted his suffering on his family because he carried too much of it to bear alone— and his family was available. He couldn't have loved us any better because he'd never found a way to love himself first.

By now, I had shed enough tears on that porch to sprout the floorboards. I went inside and dried my face. But I couldn't stop crying. I went to my photo album to find a picture of my father. I hadn't looked through that album in ages—and certainly *never* wanting to see a photo of *him*. But this night, I needed to see his face.

I finally had something to give to my father. My tears.

I found a photo of him sitting before a fake lunch counter at a photographer's shop. I didn't even think the words, but before I knew it, I'd forgiven him. I looked into his face, and I embraced him with the arms of my compassion, and all my resentment just evaporated like a fog at sunrise.

It was a tearful and freeing night.

In the days afterwards I became my father's cheerleader. I imposed myself invisibly into my memories of him. I remembered him drunk and dejected, and I imagined wrapping my arms around him and saying that everything would be all right, that I knew things were tough but that I believed in him. I envisioned him angry, spitting vile insults at my mother and at us children, and invisibly I placed a cool hand on his brow and told him I knew it wasn't us he was reviling but the cruelties of life. I relived the car ride with my mother to the south end of Georgia Street. This time I yelled through the bar's big window, "Daddy! Git yourself on home this instant! Let your family love you. At The Big House, we got plenty of love for that hungry heart of yours to feast on."

Over time, I transformed every memory of my father this way—even the worst of them. I relived, as an adult, the scenes of my childhood, and I offered understanding, mercy, and love where there had been none. I did what Nanna Eva Evaline Jessie May Mary Turner Dunn woulda done. I saw in my father the *him* that *didn't need fixing*. I retrofitted my heart with love for him.

But what saddens me to this day is knowing that only The Creator's love could have made my father feel worthy of being loved—and I never knew my father to have opened himself to *that* Love. He abused me, not because he considered me worthless and bad, but because he considered *himself* worthless and bad. The act of incest abuses two people because it's also an act of self-abuse. It's a heinous act that cuts the offender deeply and at the same time expresses his terrible grief and self-hate. To be unable to stop yourself from inflicting pain on others is devastating to the soul.

SEARCH THE FACE OF THE ONE WHO INJURED YOU.
LEARN WHAT HARM CAUSED HIM TO HARM YOU. SEE
THE SOURCE OF HIS PAIN, AND WEEP FOR HIM. WEEP FOR
YOURSELF FOR A MOMENT, BUT WEEP FOR HIM FOR DAYS.

184
▼

Arthur Lee Fountain in his late 20s.

ACROSS THE CHASM

The old cliches can't describe how forgiving my father changed my outlook on life. Sure, the grass was greener, the air was sweeter, my steps were lighter. But I felt clean and charged up like a newborn. And my heart sang songs! Songs in the morning, songs in the evening, songs in the shower, songs in the car. I whooped it up all day.

If resentment had shown in my behavior, you know that JOY did, too! I fairly bebopped down the halls at work. Idi Amin was gone, baby. Vanished. Took a boat home to Africa. For the first time ever, I felt generous toward every living soul . . . and all the dead ones, too. Generous, tolerant, patient, charitable. I forgave anything and everything that moved—*before* it moved, even. *Forgiveness in advance* was my new image.

"Go ahead," my attitude announced, "scuff my shoe, eat my candy, use up my staples, beat me to the water cooler. *Dare* to even *think* about it! *I forgive you in advance.*" Probably made people mad. They couldn't get away with nothin' because I was too quick to forgive them.

It only makes sense to bear one another's burdens—to make them light. Since we are all part of the BIG US, it frees us when we lighten each other's burdens of pain instead of heaping on more pain. When someone slaps you, look past the slap to the ignorance and the anger that caused it, knowing that:

> THE CAUSE OF ANGER AND RETALIATION IS ALWAYS PAIN. NO ONE GIVES PAIN WHO DOESN'T HAVE PAIN TO GIVE.

It is possible to act like grownups even when others act like children. To respond instead of react. To refuse to continue the cycle of pain-begetting-pain.

When I gave up wanting revenge against my father, I gave up wanting revenge against anyone. Now, I try to relieve pain where I find it. I've learned that the tears we shed for other's burdens float us easily across those chasms between people, races, even nations. When we see our enemies as burdened by hurt or ignorance, we resist hurting them or tearing them down out of bitterness. We apply mercy, as we would with little children. Even when we're forced to protect ourselves against aggression we do it with sadness for the childish ignorance behind aggression—and for the suffering that warring brings to both sides.

Not every offense comes from childish behavior. Sometimes even we adults step on one another's feet in the dance to get along with each other. But surely:

> DILIGENT CARE NOT TO HURT OTHERS AND FORGIVE-NESS WHEN OTHERS HURT US PAVE THE PATHS TO WORLD PEACE.

THE WHY OF
FORGIVENESS

M ary," I said, when the time had come for me to stand on my own, "thank you."

"M ary," I said, when the time had come for me to stand on my own, "thank you."

"You're welcome," she said.

"Good," I said. "Now you're fired!"

And we went out and celebrated over lunch.

Newfound peace, joy, and freedom are worth throwing a party for. I had learned not only how to forgive but also why to forgive.

> YOU DON'T FORGIVE FOR THE OTHER PERSON; YOU DO IT
> FOR YOU. FORGIVENESS IS A GIFT TO YOURSELF. YOU
> FOR*GIVE* TO *GET.*

And you *get* a lot!

You get healed. You get over your cravings for completeness. You get restored to yourself. You get on with your nurtured, natural life.

To resent is not natural. To let yourself heal *is.* When you

THE WHY OF
FORGIVENESS

get injured, you want the people responsible for your wound to kiss it and make it better, right? So you make sure to keep that wound open for them to see. You keep yourself from healing. After all, the more blood you can show, the bigger the kiss they'll have to lay on you! But, in my experience, people are seldom good kissers. Heck, most of the time they don't even care to see your wound. So, don't wait around, bleeding your lifeblood away. Don't hold irresponsible people responsible for fixing you. Only The Creator can fix you perfectly. When you trust in him to make things right, forgiveness is easy. You'll do it for your own health.

And you'll rejoice in your independence. Believe me—until you forgive, you are *dependent* on the object of your bitterness. You depend on it to make you happy because you've given it the power to make you miserable. You depend on it for your success because you blame it for your failure. You depend on it to give you peace of mind because you allow it to make you afraid.

188
▼

UNSHACKLE YOURSELF! YOUR WILL IS YOUR OWN. TRUE INDEPENDENCE IS TO BE EXCUSE FREE.

We *get* so much by forgiving, it's odd we consider having to do it unfair. We think *fair* is when the other guy hurts as much as we do. I got angry because my father had died before I could really sock it to him. You know, an eye for an eye. I didn't know that he had hurt himself worse than he had ever hurt me. This doesn't mean that we have to grant amnesty to evil. Evil actions deserve a just punishment. But the punishment should never come out of bitter retribution. It should never give us prideful satisfaction to see another person destroyed by the consequences of his or her own destructive acts. Compassion is the only way to lasting peace.

LAW REQUIRES JUSTICE. LOVE REQUIRES FORGIVENESS. WE MUST TRY TO DO BOTH TOGETHER. THAT WAY, WHEN JUSTICE CAN'T BE SERVED, WE OURSELVES ARE NOT DESTROYED.

Forgiveness sets us free from the heavy responsibility of passing judgment and of inflicting punishment upon things that will be forever beyond our control to change. When we forgive, we begin focusing on what it is that makes us grow instead of what it is that holds us back.

I continue to forgive my father because I still struggle at times with the effects of his behavior on me. That's just the way life is. After a hard day, sometimes the thing I want to do the most is to call the pizza guy and yell into the phone, "Get yourself over here, *now*! I want an extra-large, extra-everything—and don't bother to slice it. Just fold it up, and I'll say AH!"

We can never be free from all the ripples of our hard experiences, but we can always choose to forgive. People make mistakes, but committing to love means committing to forgive—*over and over*. That's what love does. We'll never have chasms too difficult to cross if we're quick to forgive. Forgiveness is a miracle balm that binds us fast to one another. The instructions on the label say "Apply immediately and liberally." It's only difficult to forgive when we haven't discovered what a precious gift forgiving is.

Now, a word to those who currently suffer ongoing abuse. Forgiveness does not mean you must stick with someone who continues to hurt you. Say, "I love you and I forgive you, but I

189
▼

won't allow you to hurt me again." Then make tracks. Don't be afraid. Find someone who will love you better. Someone who has integrity enough to respect you no matter what burdens of pain they bear. Do what you must do to release yourself, and then go your way in peace. Forgiving someone does not make that person innocent of a crime. It makes you innocent of holding a grudge. If you refuse to carry anger or bitter pride an abundant new life will open up to you.

To turn your heart against no person is a universal law which, when obeyed, brings the richness of universal rewards.

And *that's* the Why of Forgiveness.

ABUNDANT REWARDS

I remember the day I realized that, for the first time ever, nothing could hold me back, that I had at last become fully myself and fully alive. It was in the year 1990 A.F. (After Forgiving). I was in a hardware store: the Lumberjack in Sacramento. I went there to buy a hammer and some little tacks 'cause I had some stuff to hang on my walls at home. (This is when that *wall thing* got started. My walls had been pretty much naked before. When scarcity's your lifestyle, it shows up in your interior design.)

Anyway, I selected a hammer (all-steel, one-piece construction, rubber grip handle) and some little tacks, and I took them up to the front of the Lumberjack store to pay for them. The cashier—her name was Donna—totaled up my purchase, took my twenty-dollar bill, and handed me my change.

Then it happened.

She smiled at me and said some words that I will never ever forget as long as I live. She said, "Thanks for shopping at Lumberjack. Your receipt's in the bag."

Wow! Incredible. Ten little words and a smile. That's all it took to wake me up. Donna was speaking to *me*, I realized, and smiling at *me*. I was all present and accounted for—no pieces of me missing or distracted or obscured.

"Oh," I said, "you're very welcome. And Donna, you have a *great* smile!"

"Thanks," she beamed.

And that was it. I walked out of the Lumberjack with everything I needed to redecorate my house as well as to redirect my life. Good timing, because a weakening economy would shortly shut down the Obesity Recovery Clinic. Shortly after my trip to the Lumberjack, I lost my job.

No problem, I thought. A dynamic, college-educated, African-American lady with good credentials ought to be able to find work easily.

Didn't happen. No jobs anywhere. I was on unemployment and even tried to get work processing unemployment applications! Didn't happen.

But something *did* happen soon. I continued to speak on occasion to groups who remembered me from Joan Fountain's Body and Soul. I had given up that business when my job at the Clinic became too demanding. But now, I needed the money, so I agreed to speak a few times until I found regular work. And, since I'm an honest person, I reported every dollar I earned to the unemployment office.

The first time I reported, the clerk was astonished. "*How* much did you say you earned?" she asked, and I repeated, "Two thousand." Then she wanted to know how many days it took to earn the two thousand, and I told her. "One." This astonished her even more, and she wanted to know what I did to earn *that* much in a day. I answered, "I'm a speaker." It took having to repeat those words many times over the weeks before I finally paid attention to them. "I'm a speaker." "I'm a speaker." "I'm a speaker . . ."

"Hey! *I'm a speaker!*"

And once I declared it, I became it.

I went right out and got some business cards and letterhead stating: *Joan Fountain, Consulting, Training, and Keynote Speaker.* Soon I was working an average of twenty days a month. I haven't looked back since, except to appreciate the miracles along the way. The experts never guessed the true reason the national economy went into decline that year. It was so that I would lose my job and God could get his message through to me, telling me where I belonged.

To simplify the events of my life: first I discovered truth, then I accepted truth, then I forgave. And I *finally* got to "duh!" I found out who I am and why I'm here. Self-knowledge is one of the rewards forgiving brings. Of course we're all a part of the BIG US and that includes God, so:

193
▼

SELF-KNOWLEDGE IS TO KNOW THE CREATOR IN US.

Over time, I came to know The Creator in me. I learned that when I trust only Him to guide my career, and when I speak for the purpose of nurturing others, my work feeds me. It becomes my air, my water, my food, my lover, my friend, my comfort. It takes away all the cravings I've ever felt and fills me to overflowing. My work answers why angels have attended my life. Nurturing is my purpose and I do it best when I speak to groups.

I believe that everyone's purpose is to nurture because that's the purpose of the universe. Each of us must discover how we nurture best and then magnify that in ourselves. When we do, nothing can prevent the rewards of abundance and joy and serenity from showering over our heads.

WHEN WE NURTURE, WE ARE NURTURED.

CRYSTAL WORDS OF WISDOM

Have you ever had the feeling that huge chunks of yourself are missing somehow? As if you've been used as chum for the sharks? That you just can't nurture anybody because, after the feeding frenzy, what's left of you is just too shredded to offer any nurturing? I know that feeling—I *know* that feeling.

Some folks, when they feel chewed up by life, lapse into a walking coma. They seem alive, but in reality they are *sleeping life off*. They are so sensitive to the hardships of living that they resist waking up to life. These people show vital signs, but they possess no vitality.

Others turn frantic and obsess with stuff they think will make them whole again. These people can't nurture others—not because they don't have the heart for it, like the walking-coma people, but because they're too busy nurturing themselves, trying to get what they feel life owes them. They think they have to be smarter, faster, richer, sexier, healthier, busier than somebody else to feel complete. They focus on their bodies, their clothes, their images. Their motto is—you've heard it before—"Living well is the best revenge."

Still others belong to a third group—the ones who feel so betrayed by the hardships of life that they practice "get the other guy before he gets you." It's a way of life that is spreading alarmingly in this world. Self-preservation at any cost is the new creed. Pick your turf, resent the world, arm yourself up the wahzoo, and dominate by destroying. Street gangs and some corporate leaders share the tip of this iceberg.

So. When life gives you a boo-boo, do you beat a retreat, nurse your wounds, feel sorry for yourself, and never come out to play again? Or do you charge out there and battle for retribution against the SOB (Something Offensive that Bites) that stuck it to you? Or do you think you can put up walls and let no one in or dodge boo-boos by boo-booing everyone else first?

No! No! Hear me say it louder. *NO!*

STOP REFUSING TO LIVE, AND **STOP** REFUSING TO LET LIVE.

It's a life-nurturing universe we belong to. Stop resenting that to be nurtured can hurt. You've heard of *growing pains*. They are real! Experiences that help us grow are often painful and frightening. But try to see them for the good they bring, and never stop trusting them.

To teach her babies to fly, a mother bird pushes them out of the nest. During their plunge to the pavement, the birdies may squabble over which one of them should take the blame for ticking Mom off. Or they may scratch and claw at one another and try not to end up on the pavement as the birdie on the bottom who softens the blow for the others. Or the birdies may go limp and take the plunge, knowing that ending up as birdie roadkill was their fate all along. Or they could use their predicament as an opportunity to test the laws of birdie physics, spread their wings, and fly.

Which of these behaviors shows resentment at being pushed out of the nest? Which of them shows gratitude for a boot in the birdie behind?

Like birds that will never fly if they resent the chance to try, we will never grow if we resent the opportunities that challenges and hardship afford.

Adversity is God's classroom. That first stab of discomfort is the school bell telling you class is in session. A wise student walks in and says, "There's a lesson here for me. I need to sit down and shut up till I get it." Somebody else whines and cries, "Aw, *hell*. How come I got to be in *here* again. I'm here all the time!" Another body tries to make an issue out of it. "My people are in school every day!" they complain. "And those *other* people, *they* don't have to go to school. That's not fair!"

Fight and kick and hate it all you want. It's your choice how long you stay in misery. Learn the lesson, and you can leave school early that day. Don't pay attention, throw spitwads, procrastinate your homework, resent The Teacher, and you'll stay late.

The reason we're on this campus is to learn about ourselves so that we'll make the most efficient use of our infinite gifts and rise toward our infinite potential. But we are multifaceted, complicated Eds and coEds. It's impossible to learn everything at once. That's why we should thank our Wise Teacher for His curriculum of adversity.

ADVERSITY, WHEN SEEN AS A BLESSING, HELPS US CONSIDER OURSELVES ONE FACET AT A TIME. THROUGH THE PROCESS OF ELIMINATION IN OUR STRUGGLES, WE FIGURE OUT WHAT'S TRUE ABOUT OURSELVES AND WHAT IS NOT.

My momma used to make apricot jam—thick, sweet, taste bud-exploding apricot jam. We picked the fruit for her, leaving on the tree any fruit with even a hint of green flesh. Momma demanded only the ripest, the sweetest apricots we could find for her jam. She drenched the fruit with icy water in the kitchen sink, cleaned it, and took out the pits. Then into a big steel pot the apricots went and onto the stove, where the steady blue flame of a burner turned the juicy fruit into jam. Momma always let her jam simmer extra long, until what she finally poured into the jars was the truest essence, the purest flavor, the genuine soul of those apricots.

Adversity is our steady and refining flame. It burns away all that's nonessential in us, leaving behind just the good stuff, the genuine stuff, the powerful core of us. And *my*, are we ever *delicious*! We have to let that fire do its work. If we resent it, we turn ourselves away not only from the benefit of its heat but also from the benefit of its light.

197
▼

Sometimes we *do* feel that life takes big chunks out of us. But maybe we're better off without those particular chunks. Our stubborn attempts at restoring ourselves can be more destructive than helpful. Our deepest selves suffer when we hold tightly to the way things "ought to have been." The way things "were" or "ought to have been" is not the way things *are*. Our depressions, anxieties, and stresses are self-inflicted when we refuse the simple cure: *Let it be.*

I know. We hate to let our pain be. But our pain is part of us and we need to find something *nurturing* to do with it instead of something hurtful. Then we'll grow. God is in loving control of every situation and event, even the ones we've never been able to make sense of. It is best to learn what we can from what we'd rather resent and then let it be. Let it be part of that Love which makes everything fair and equal and true. And soon you'll understand that:

> IN LIFE, THERE IS NO NEED TO FORGIVE GOD FOR OUR CIRCUMSTANCES. THERE IS NOTHING TO RESENT. EVERY CIRCUMSTANCE IS PERFECT IN ITS POTENTIAL TO HELP US GROW.

To accept that NOTHING BAD HAPPENS, EVER, one has to come to an understanding of what living is all about. If living is acquiring wisdom and depth of soul and unconditional love for others, then how can the loss of material things or or the loss of a job, or your health, be bad? Or even the loss of a loved one? No quantity of loss destroys our ability to gain quality of soul.

> DO WITH YOUR PAIN THAT WHICH NURTURES THE SOUL, AND ADVERSITY WILL NOT DIMINISH BUT MAGNIFY YOU.

SAY THE SIMPLE THINGS

I got on the phone one night. "Hello, Momma," I said. "I just signed my first big contract!"

"To do what?"

"To *speak*, Momma. I told you I speak in public, now."

"You have to sign a contract to speak?"

"Yes, so that my client knows what he's getting, and I know what he's paying me for."

"People *pay you* to speak?"

"Yeah. More than I thought I could ask for!"

"Why don't you get a *real* job?" Momma asked. "I don't understand."

"I tell people things they feel have value. It *is* a real job. And I feel really good doing it, too. I wish you'd come and hear me sometime."

"I've heard you talk lots."

"Momma, I don't *talk*, I *speak*. Get the difference."

This was amazing! Momma was saying enough that I could actually *argue* with her!

"So what do you *speak* about?" she asked.

"Things like how to find the silver linings, how to be your best, how to always love somebody no matter what. You know, stuff I learned from you."

She was silent.

"Momma?" I said.

"From me?" she asked.

"Of *course*. Who else? You were a good teacher."

She was silent again.

"You gave us a good example, Momma," I added. "You *did*."

"I did what I had to do," she said.

Now it was my turn to be silent. I felt Momma might be trying to apologize in some way. I didn't need her apology, but I did need to let her know I had forgiven her.

"I know you did, Momma," I said. "I understand. It's okay."

Simple words. They're all that's needed to make a start. To shift things from shadow to light. To make someone feel you setting them free. To let yourself out from under the burden of keeping someone in your debt. To show just the tip of new possibilities in love.

READ THIS LAST

Over time, I've learned what to speak about in my new career: *myself.* Why? Because sharing my experiences can nurture others. All my adversity, every vestige of my pain can relieve the suffering of others—even if just a little. If the basic goal in life is not to hurt ourselves and not to hurt others, then the advanced goal is learning how to give everything we are, our abilities, our time, our possessions, our joys and our sorrows for the good of others. When we do that, Hallelujah!—all the walls come down. We become limitless in who we are and in what we can achieve. The better we nurture, the more we become like The Creator—The Perfect and Limitless Nurturer.

On those rare nights when I can bear to set aside my busyness, when I drive myself out of the city to find a hill with a patch of soft grass, when I lay my back against Our Mother Planet and set my face toward the stars of Our Father Universe, I get a funny feeling that The Big Guy has something really BIG in store for those who become loving and merciful as he is. A permanent, glorious home. A place among beings of light. A new beginning to the sacred cycle of The Nurtured Becoming Nurturer. An eternal and happy time when everything is Love, everything is Joy, everything is Truth, everything is Serenity, and when EVERYTHING GOOD HAPPENS, ALWAYS.

My heart's greatest desire is that you and I will see each other There. But you gotta quit giving me flack about what I say and start *getting on with life*. Start loving. Start forgiving. Start living in gratitude and praise. I ain't waiting around for you *forever*, you know! All of us need to grow up and then love the one sitting next to us so he or she can grow up and love us back! We're all part of the BIG US. We've got to grow together, serve each other, and share all the abundance equally with every soul on earth.

My sweet momma, God bless her, taught me so much about love. I could have used a little more of it from her in my life— true—but I know she loved me as best she could. What happened at The Big House must have been hard to understand and to deal with. I can't blame Momma for being unsure over how to share her love. Anyway, my cravings for her affection taught me the importance and the power of a mother's love. There's a mighty virtue in it, I'll tell you. The little shows of affection I got from her during her last years came straight from the powers of heaven itself. It felt mighty wonderful.

Momma was plugged in. I know it.

Remember what I wrote about the day she died? How I saw her dancing with my father in the spirit and how I felt the rush of her joy at being in his arms. What I didn't write was how hard I cried that rainy day. How deeply I wished that, in life, Momma could have been as free in her joy and her love for me as I saw she was for my father in the spirit. I'd been grieving my whole life for want of a mother's love. Shortly before she died, I visited her at home, wanting to give her what I had always needed to receive.

202
▼

I asked to be alone with her, and when the nurse left and the door was closed, I walked to her bedside. "Momma," I said softly. "It's me. Joan. I love you, and I'm going to miss you."

I sniffed back my tears, not wanting sadness to keep me from my purpose.

Momma needed something. I could see it in her eyes. I asked her what it was, but she was too weak to speak. She put her hands in her hair and began pulling at it as if she wanted it brushed.

"No way would you have ever let me do this before," I said to her. I went to her dresser and took out her hairbrush. Then I leaned over Momma and held her in my arms while I brushed out her hair. And for the first time since I was eight, I freely shared my love and my affection with my mother—along with lots of tears. Tears of love and of joy.

I felt one with her in love that day. I felt her a part of me and me a part of her. She seemed so present within me that I couldn't tell where she left off and I began. My efforts to freely express my love overcame all the barriers between us. At last.

It bothered me that my momma was never able to travel and hear me speak. Now, she can. I've felt her with me. She's in a different wrapper, but she's still my momma. And she did end up acknowledging me as a speaker. I was the only person Momma asked to speak at her funeral. It was one of the greatest honors of my life.

Like a string of pearls, we are connected to one another by more than the string: we are all of the same essence, all essential to the whole. Any sense of separateness is a lie we must move beyond. And we *must* move beyond this lie because we are each more miraculous than a pearl, each more worthy of being treasured and cherished and loved beyond measure. To

203
▼

consider any one of us as less than another, or to withhold ourselves or any of our love, diminishes the whole and denies the truth of who we are.

WE ARE LOVING CREATORS IN INFANCY. THERE EXIST WHOLE UNIVERSES OF POTENTIAL INSIDE OF US, INFINITE GENERATIONS OF LIFE, AND A BOUNDLESS CAPACITY TO LOVE.

When you yourself are freed from the obstacles of error, ignorance, and bitterness, turn outward and free a fellow human being. Teach someone else that NOTHING BAD HAPPENS, EVER. Choosing to reach out will transform our world—dark to light. Anger to forgiveness. Violence to peace. Injury to renewal. Enmity to love. Guilt to freedom. Fear to strength. And sorrow to joy.

When enough of us come together, when we hold one another openly and learn to become of one heart, one mind, and one life, there will be unleashed a power and a light that will wipe out all the effects of chaos and hardship and disunity in this world. And oh, the LOVE we'll share *then*! The Creator of All will say, "Hey. Welcome home! There will be no more sorrow, no more pain. You've already learned those lessons well. I told you NOTHING BAD HAPPENS, EVER!"

THE QUALITY OF MERCY IS NOT STRAIN'D
IT DROPPETH AS THE GENTLE RAIN FROM HEAVEN
UPON THE PLACE BENEATH. IT IS TWICE BLEST:
IT BLESSETH HIM THAT GIVES AND HIM THAT TAKES.

William Shakespeare,
The Merchant of Venice